Tim Keep knows fthe goodness of G
both attempt great ₁ ₋ ₋₋ ₋ ᵣ ₋₋₋ ₅ ₋₋₋₋ ₋₋₋₋ ᵢ ₋ ₋₋₋ ₋ᵢ₋ᵢₑₛ ₁ ₁ ₀ ₁ ₁ ₁
Him. If you take to heart the wisdom Tim unpacks in *Keep It Simple*, and if every day you practice just a little bit more of that wisdom, your life will be filled with the peaceful fruit of righteousness. Read this book; let it inspire you as it did me. Pray over its pearls of wisdom, talk it over with dear friends, share it with people longing to make a difference in a broken world. You'll be glad you did!

— Dean Davis
Architect, New Village Church Planting Program, One Mission Society

In *Keep It Simple,* Tim Keep offers readers the profound grasp of "heart truth"—simple and pure! It is this grand simplicity of soul, this utter honesty of heart, this keen purity of purpose, this ultimate gaze on God that will truly open our lives to the Holy Spirit's usefulness. This book has challenged me, convicted me and captivated me. Its stories and candid narratives will open to you the wonder of hard but glorious "heart truth." This book is not for the superficial believer who is content with any meager amount of spirituality. It is for parents, leaders, true believers in every walk of life, who will embrace the rugged romance of fully yielding to God's leadership. Here is the grand simplicity of Christ, is the answer to our frantic and sometimes failing Kingdom efforts.

— Rev. Blake Jones
General Secretary, The Bible Methodist Connection of Churches

Of books on leadership there is no end, but a book like *Keep It Simple* is a rare find. Tim moves beyond the mechanical principles often on display in leadership books and gives us the simple foundational truths that will help an honest Christian worker be effective for God and His Kingdom. He carefully points out that real leadership is built on character, and character is born from the seedbed of biblical conviction and common sense! This book is a must-read for Christian leaders.
— **Dr. Michael Avery**
Chancellor, God's Bible School and College

Simplicity is the hallmark of God's interaction with man. Tim Keep captures this powerful principle as he openly shares personal experiences and draws from scripture to probe key leadership and relationship principles. With straightforward simplicity, *Keep It Simple* distills Christian leadership into its essential elements, while exposing the pitfalls that trip well-meaning people along the way. Whether just starting on the Christian leadership journey, or desiring to deepen your understanding as a leader, or to gain fresh insight into relationships, you will be challenged and enriched by this timely and well-written book.
— **Will Byler**
President, Mission Helps

Tim Keep writes not only from years of observation and ministry practice, but also from much prayer and reflection and thoughts gleaned from examples as diverse as Brengle and Bonhoeffer. Any ministry leader, whether action-oriented or contemplative by nature, will find in *Keep It Simple* a balanced description of ministry that is both visionary and rooted in a deep relationship with God.
— **Dr. Steve Gibson**
President, Evangelistic Faith Missions

Against the backdrop of stories from Job, Daniel and the Gospels and from his own spiritual journey as a missionary, husband, and father Tim develops ten "simple", foundational principles for developing the character and habits of a spiritual leader. If you are on the climb toward spiritual maturity, one of Tim's candid life stories in *Keep It Simple* may just help you past your next hard place. Highly recommended for a Christian of any age or for a ten week group study.
— **David Eslinger**
Businessman, Teacher

Keep It Simple is full of practical wisdom for young leaders who want to plant their lives in Christ and see what His resurrected life can do through humble, obedient people who dare to depend on the Holy Spirit. As someone who was privileged to serve under Tim Keep's leadership for 12 years as a missionary, I can tell you that he practices the principles you will read about here.
— **Dr. Richard Hutchison**
Director, Bible Methodist Missions

Most often ministry effectiveness is forged in the battleground of personal spiritual growth. In *Keep It Simple* missionary leader, Tim Keep, shares passionately and vulnerably the lessons he has learned in 30 plus years of ministry that have enabled him to effectively serve as a pastor, missionary, mission director, and now president of Shepherds Global Classroom. This is not a 10-step book to ministry effectiveness, but timeless lessons learned "in the gym" of spiritual growth and discipline that will help any ministry leader as they strive to live and lead like Christ.
— **Harold Martin**
President, FEA Ministries

In recent years, many people have been deeply hurt by the failure of some well-known evangelical leaders. How I wish those leaders had read (and followed) *Keep It Simple!* Yes, these principles are simple but they are immensely important. Tim illustrates these biblical principles with examples drawn from a lifetime of fruitful ministry. I highly recommend this practical and insightful book to young pastors and church leaders.
— **Dr. Randal McElwain**
Director of Global Training, Shepherds Global Classroom

TIM KEEP
with Becky Keep

KEEP IT SIMPLE

Reflections on the Character, Habits, and Practices of Christians Who Lead

Copyright © 2023 by Tim Keep and Becky Keep

All rights reserved. No part of this publication may be reproduced, distributed, or transmitted in any form or by any means, including photocopying, recording, or other electronic or mechanical methods, without the prior written permission of the publisher, except as permitted by U.S. copyright law.

Published by Whispering Pines Publishing, Shoals, Indiana.

Unless otherwise indicated, scripture quotations are from the ESV® Bible (The Holy Bible, English Standard Version®), copyright © 2001 by Crossway, a publishing ministry of Good News Publishers. Used by permission. All rights reserved. The ESV text may not be quoted in any publication made available to the public by a Creative Commons license. The ESV may not be translated in whole or in part into any other language.

Printed and bound in Shoals, Indiana by Country Pines Printing, Inc.

Set in EB Garamond
Designed by Shane Muir Design

To purchase additional copies of this book, or to see other titles from the authors, visit www.beckykeep.com

ISBN: 978-1-948362-77-1

Printed in the United States of America

10 9 8 7 6 5 4 3 2 1

To my friend and brother, Rev. David Yucaddi, a humble man who's had an enormous impact on the way I think, on the way I live, and on the way I lead. I am forever grateful.

1 Corinthians 1:26–29

CONTENTS

Introduction — 11

Chapter 1—A SIMPLE PURSUIT — 17
Let's talk about the thing that's more important than working miracles and casting out demons.

Chapter 2—A SIMPLE FOCUS ON JESUS — 37
Let's talk about becoming what you behold.

Chapter 3—A SIMPLE GOSPEL — 55
Let's talk about preaching the gospel to yourself every day.

Chapter 4—A SIMPLE COMMITMENT TO INTEGRITY — 75
Let's talk about living authentically.

Chapter 5—A SIMPLE DISCIPLINE — 95
Let's talk about getting in the gym.

Chapter 6—A SIMPLE HUMILITY 115
Let's talk about getting over ourselves.

Chapter 7—A SIMPLE WORK ETHIC 137
Let's talk about working hard.

Chapter 8—A SIMPLE VISION 159
Let's talk about knowing where you're going.

Chapter 9—A SIMPLE LOVE 179
Let's talk about how you're going to treat people.

Chapter 10—A SIMPLE FRIENDSHIP 199
Let's talk about my friend David, and why you need someone like him in your life.

Notes 223

INTRODUCTION

EARLY MONDAY MORNING, June 6th, 2022, I awoke in Puerto Escondido, Mexico, to a gorgeous sunrise. I found myself in a reflective mood because today was an important day. Today marked the last day of my final overseas trip as Director of Missions for a fellowship of churches Becky and I have been privileged to belong to for many years—The Bible Methodist Connection of Churches. And I knew that very soon we would conclude our twenty-sixth and final year of missionary service with this organization as well—thirteen of those years in the Philippine Islands. The Lord was clearly leading us to a full-time leadership role with Shepherds Global Classroom, and the transition was only days away.

My room faced east that morning, overlooking the crystal blue waters of the Puerto Bay. My Scripture reading was from Psalm 78; and as I read these words, I thought of how profoundly blessed we'd been to do such meaningful work for so many years: "In spite of all this, they still sinned; despite his wonders, they did not believe. So, he made their days vanish like a breath (NKJV reads, "their days he consumed with futility"), and their years in terror" (Psalm 78:32-33).

As I looked out over the bay, observing the changing colors of the sunrise and watching fishermen in the distance struggle to pull their boats ashore after a night on the water, I wrote these reflections in my journal:

> I can think of no greater judgment than that my life would be consumed in futility; that I would wake up every day without vision, without direction, without good work to accomplish, without hope for the future, without the knowledge that we, with our spiritual siblings all over the world, are building the eternal kingdom of God. Nor can I imagine living in constant fear—even "terror"—of what might happen to me or my family. Futility and fear: these were the judgments Israel received because of their unbelief.
>
> Faith demonstrated in obedience is the key to a life filled with meaning and purpose. And the fruit of obedience is a sense of security—of being guided, cared for, and protected. This is what every believer has discovered. These are God's greatest gifts!
>
> Today I end my final out-of-country travel for Bible Methodist Missions. For twenty-six years Becky and I have watched God do amazing, even supernatural things through simple trust and obedience—things we would have never experienced had we given in to fear. But one of the greatest gifts God has given these many years is

simply a sense of purpose. We, though so ordinary and flawed, have gotten to wake up every day to pursue a vision of eternal significance. Thank you, Father!

There was yet another final event which happened on that trip as well: after twenty-six years of doing life and ministry in a cross-cultural context, I delivered my *final message* for Bible Methodist Missions, delivered through an interpreter to the students of Ezra Biblical Seminary.

The setting was picturesque. Seminary students and their families gathered under a pavilion situated on top of a grassy knoll, beside a cool, clear mountain stream just outside the southern Mexico town of San Gabriel. I thought and prayed a lot over the message and decided to share a summary of the most important lessons I'd learned over nearly three decades of Christian ministry. I called these, "Ten Commandments for Christian Workers," as a way to *hopefully* make them memorable; and these are the simple "principles" I want to share in this book.

I chose the title *Keep it Simple* because, while there are many pressures and complexities to life in the modern world, the pathway of divine favor—to a fruitful life and ministry—is still simple. I did not say "easy," but "simple." It isn't complicated.

The psalmist expressed this principle of simplicity when he asked, rhetorically, "Who shall ascend the hill of the LORD? And who shall stand in his holy place?" The answer is simple, "He who has clean hands and a pure heart, who does not lift up his soul to what is false and does not swear deceitfully. He will receive blessing from the LORD" (Psalm 24:3-5).

The prophet Micah expressed this principle of simplicity in his day of complexities when he wrote, "He has told you, O man, what is good; and what does the LORD require of you but to do justice, and to love kindness, and to walk humbly with your God?" (Micah 6:8).

Jesus expressed it in these words, "And he answered, 'You shall love the Lord your God with all your heart and with all your soul and with all your strength and with all your mind, and your neighbor as yourself'" (Luke 10:27).

More importantly, Jesus modeled a simple life and ministry. Jesus certainly understood the complexities of life. But somehow, even while political, religious, and social battles were raging all around him, he managed a life of simplicity. He practiced solitude, he prayed, he practiced restraint, he tuned out distractions and stayed focused on the will of God. He focused on his work. He worked in the power of the Spirit. He was present for the person right in front of him. He made disciples. He said "no" to himself. He picked up his cross. And walked with the Father. It wasn't easy, but Jesus kept it simple.

None of the simple principles I talk about in the following pages will come to you *naturally,* but through the gracious work of God's indwelling presence. We can only keep it simple as we stay in the presence of Jesus and yield daily to the purifying, teaching, training, empowering ministry of the indwelling Holy Spirit.

This little book is written especially for young men and women whom God has gifted and called to lead the church around the world. I do not apologize for its simplicity. I simply want to help you to become all that God desires you to become and to find your place in God's kingdom...with joy! I want to help you as I have been helped by Jesus and so many of his choicest friends—my parents and siblings, Bible school professors, my lovely wife, friends and family, fellow ministers, missionary colleagues, brothers and sisters from other nations (especially the Philippines where we were honored to serve for thirteen years), Christian leaders with incredible stature, and, most importantly, a humble man named David whom I will talk about in the final chapter. Without a doubt, this friend and brother has helped form my understanding of spiritual things more than any other.

The simple thoughts expressed in these pages began to take shape years ago as Becky and I worked through the challenges of cross-cultural ministry among people now dear to our hearts. When I knew our time there was coming to a close, I spent countless hours in a little office next to our mission house writing down some of the most important lessons God has taught us throughout our years there. I've drawn from many of those writings for this book.

I'm excited to explore my top ten list of simple but vital principles for effective Christian leadership with you now. Thank you for joining me on this journey.

CHAPTER 1

A SIMPLE PURSUIT

Let's talk about the thing that's more important than working miracles and casting out demons.

> "God is most glorified in us when we are most satisfied in him." — John Piper

KNOWING GOD MUST BE THE FIRST PURSUIT of a Christian leader. It's that simple.

Leading is not first. Reading is not first. Preaching or teaching is not first. Nor is serving the poor, praying for the sick, or casting out demons! Being with God and knowing him is first. As Paul expressed it, "Indeed, I count everything as loss because of the surpassing worth of knowing Christ Jesus my Lord. For his sake I have suffered the loss of all things and count them as rubbish, in order that I may gain Christ" (Philippians 3:8).

The current president of Moody Bible Institute, Mark Jobe, recounts a pivotal moment in his early Christian life. He had attended Moody Bible Institute, but dropped out after a year and began to flounder, wondering what he would do with his life.

Mark decided to spend the summer in southern France, not far from where he'd grown up as a missionary kid. He worked in a little hotel, all the while asking himself, "What's my purpose? What am I going to throw my life and energy into?"

Before Mark had left Chicago, someone had given him a little booklet called, *The Knowledge of the Holy*, by A.W. Tozer. In a sermon to students at Moody, Mark recounts,

> I was shocked by the fact that Tozer kept saying, "You need to know God." And I was thinking, "No, I need to know my purpose, my job, my career!" And A.W. Tozer kept saying, "You need to know God! You need to know God! You need to know God! The center of your existence is your relationship with God. When you get that right then everything else in life begins to align itself; but if that is not in its place, then everything is out of alignment." [1]

Mark continues,

> Something happened that summer. I started worrying less about what I was going to do after I graduated from school, and I started to think more about knowing God. I came back to Moody, and I was different. Because I didn't just come back using Moody as a platform for my next season of life. I came back saying, "No, I'm going to use this time to know God."

The knowledge of God will be the key to everything. Knowing God will be the key to your effectiveness as a Christian and as a spiritual leader.

Knowing God will be the key to your patience when discipleship is costly and ministry painful. It will be the key to your satisfaction, your confidence, your boldness, your obedience, your steadfastness, and the depth and quality of your love. The knowledge of God will enable you to know and respect yourself and others. And in the pursuit of God you will discover your purpose.

Many centuries before Paul wrote those famous words in Philippians 3:8, Moses found himself in a very difficult position. God had called him to lead the Israelites out of Egyptian enslavement and into the Promised Land. But now Moses is hearing God say something very disturbing: "Go up to a land flowing with milk and honey; but I will not go up among you, lest I consume you on the way, for you are a stiff-necked people" (Exodus 33:3).

What?! This can't be!

Moses can't accept this terrifying proposal. He can't imagine an Israel without God. He can't imagine leading without God. If not God, then who would deliver Israel from trouble? Who would defend them? Who would fight their battles? Who would provide bread? Who would quench their thirst? Who would heal their sicknesses? Who would lead them into the land? *What will distinguish them from every other nation on earth, if not God?!* (Exodus 33:16).

You know the story. God relents and decides to go up with Moses and Israel after all, but I'm intrigued by the reason God gives for this "change" of heart: "And the LORD said to Moses, 'This very thing that you have spoken I will do, for you have found favor in my sight, and I know you by name'" (Exodus 33:17). With this astounding statement, God portrays himself as one who can be persuaded, *through friendship,* to do what he otherwise would not do.

If you really want to be a spiritual leader, then I need you to think about something: Like Moses, you are going to find yourself in some impossible situations—situations where if God doesn't show up you're never going to make it. What will you do then? I'll tell you what we *all* must do. We must become friends of God! We must cultivate a relationship with the beautiful God Moses came to know and love. We must know his name, and he must know ours. Within that relationship is every possibility you will ever need!

I am convinced there is *nothing...nothing* God wills to do that he cannot or will not do through that person who makes God his friend!

Knowing God is the key to everything we will *become* and everything we will ever *do as servants of God*. This is the lesson the Lord began to teach me in my first faltering foray into Christian ministry.

How well I remember our first three-and-a-half-year ministry "crucible." After graduating from Bible college in Florida, Becky and I moved 1,376 miles north to western Michigan to assume our first pastoral assignment, trading the warm Atlantic Ocean for beautiful but cold Lake Michigan. We moved into a lovely parsonage and began shepherding a small—very small—wounded, and somewhat cynical congregation. By cynical I mean that a few painful experiences with pastors in the past, as well as some of their own foolish choices, had left their faith more than a little damaged. They had heard about every pastoral "vision" imaginable, and I would soon learn they were not going to be easily impressed by one more!

I was very young, not overly confident, and a little intimidated by this ministry launch, but there was a measure of excitement in it too, for both Becky and me. Four years of biblical instruction had helped me become more biblically literate, had given me a strong doctrinal framework, and had produced in me a love for the Word of God. Becky had completed nursing school, was growing in her faith, and was a loving and attentive mother to our firstborn, Valerie.

During the four years in Florida, we had both been profoundly impacted by authentic, Christ-centered teachers and mentors. We were full of passion and had come to believe that with the *Spirit working through us* we could make a difference for Jesus in this new place. And the Lord did use us. Some converted and discipled under our ministry in those early years are already in heaven, and others are faithfully following Jesus today. But progress was slow and painful.

Week after week I prepared sermons, visited members, and tried to reach out to new people; but I was self-conscious, and the outreach part did *not* come naturally to me. And there was the fact that while I was passionate for truth, I could be short on grace. I knew far too little of Jesus' kindness and gentleness for myself to share with others. I was also idealistic and awkward, and while the church began to grow a little, I was still nervous, restless, anxious.

My very first journal entry on June 30th, 1993, reads, "The best word which describes the way I feel at this moment is *'overwhelmed!'* Overwhelmed by the tremendous responsibility of everyone looking to me as their leader. Overwhelmed by the (largeness) of the task—where do I start?" I was just 23 years old.

Throughout that first year, I continued to record a variety of thoughts, experiences, and emotions. Here is a slightly edited sampling:

> I'm ashamed to say it, but these people don't motivate me much...! (Can you say, "Childish!")

The thing that really overwhelms me is not just the tremendous responsibility, but also the lost feeling of not knowing where to start.... Another thing hard to get used to is the fact that I'm my own boss. When going through college I had such a structured lifestyle. My day was full of school and work and studies and Christian service....

All these feelings have really caused me to cry out to God and to ask him to guide every step.... I want him to bring people into my life and to expand his work as he sees fit. Please Lord, enable me to keep motivated and focused... straighten out my wrong thinking and unreasonable expectations, but keep me challenged...!

I've been having a great time studying God's Word and reading good books. The books I've been reading are: *They Found the Secret,* Raymond Edman; *The Knowledge of the Holy,* A.W. Tozer; *The Apostle,* John Pollock; *These Earthen Vessels,* W.T. Purkiser.... In the midst of the good things God is doing in me I still have this restless feeling that I'm not doing enough.... I want to be more than busy—I want to be used of God.

These days are strange. I'm up, then down; totally overwhelmed, then free. I can't figure it out.... I constantly walk around with a huge knot in my stomach.... I must have some relief.... "Lord, teach me through all of this that I am dependent on you, and may I never forget these times and who I am." I love Christ so much.... I need him more than I can express.

> The Lord is teaching me how important my family is. I want to love Becky more, as well as Valerie. I love that girl so much sometimes I almost burst! I hope she loves me as much. I laid my hands on her the other night as she slept... and committed her totally to God.

I was a young man in turmoil.

A couple of weeks into ministry I decided one evening to visit our neighbors. (I'm not sure where Becky was, but it would have been wise to take her along!) I recorded my frustration:

> Today I went to meet my neighbors. This turned out to be very *unfulfilling*. One guy was an alcoholic... though kind. The next guy barely said, "Hello." Another neighbor told me to come back another day.... I went across the street and met a friendly lady (who) told me her son was outside. I tried to be very friendly and to introduce myself to him, but he didn't say anything, so I went on. I met a very nice young woman who was *very friendly*... The next house, though, took all the wind out of my sails. I told the "gentleman" who I was, that I was just out to meet my neighbors, and introduced myself as the new minister from the church across the street. He told me to *"Go away!" "Get out!"* I did! Oh, I almost forgot, even the nice people remarked that I didn't look old enough to be out of high school. I think I'll go to bed; it's been a long day.

On another occasion I introduced myself to yet another neighbor and was taken aback when she exclaimed. "Oh, you're from that church that was in the newspaper!" Seeing my clueless expression, she filled me in on the details. There had been an ugly split at my little church involving a Sunday morning fist fight in the sanctuary between the pastor and a member! Much of the town had read about it. How humiliating.

My journal shows that for most of that first year of ministry, church attendance rarely got out of the teens, and this was also humiliating to me. Some of my friends who had launched into ministry the same time as I, were seeing tremendous growth. Week after week I listened to their exciting stories of leading people to Christ. I sincerely rejoiced with them but wondered what was wrong with me. I recorded these thoughts: "I think the Lord has a good reason for putting me in this position. He is teaching me to depend on him like I never have before."

> **There is much I am not satisfied with in my character and spiritual life, but I am satisfied that the Holy Spirit has uniquely formed me for a special calling, just as he has you.**
>
> *Me Too.*

Discouragement caused me to focus on myself—*my* lack of capacity (I wasn't that naturally charismatic guy and was too aware of this), *my* weaknesses and faults, *my*self compared to my friends and colleagues who were experiencing success. **The more I focused on myself, the more insecure I became.**

Unhealthy comparisons intimidated me into doing things I was not called or gifted to do. On one occasion I attended a pastors' conference where a dynamic speaker and effective outreach pastor regaled us with amazing stories of soul-winning and church growth. He and his team were filling buses and church pews. His work was exciting...impressive. And to me...impossible. But I felt guilty for not at least trying to do what he did.

One Saturday morning I went out into my community *determined* to "knock on doors" and invite people to Sunday services. All the while I was thinking to myself, *"Why is this so hard for me?!"* My introvert readers will understand.

I parked on a street a few blocks from our church and headed toward the nearest house, *secretly hoping no one would be home!* I knocked lightly, and when no one came to the door I headed for the next house, determined to grit my teeth and *do this!* This was my *job* after all... And how could I ever expect to fill the church if I didn't *do* the things a pastor is supposed to do? But no one responded to my knock in the next home, or the next home either. After knocking on three or four doors with no luck, I decided to head for home. I felt defeated and ashamed and was pretty sure God was ashamed of me too.

YOU CAN'T WEAR SAUL'S ARMOR

With almost thirty years of ministry behind me, I am much more comfortable with God's unique gifting and plan for me. There is much I am *not* satisfied with in my character and spiritual life, but I *am* satisfied that the Holy Spirit has uniquely formed me for a special calling, just as he has you. I realize that while ministry is often difficult and uncomfortable, yet it is not *ill-fitting* or *awkward.* You don't need to wear Saul's armor to slay giants. What you need is faith, and the offering to God of whatever skills he has given you.

Your maker fashioned you inside and out to fill a place no one else can fill, and he delights in his creation. He knows you by name.

He formed your desires. He gave you your talents. He even ordained your weaknesses [2]—not sins, but weaknesses or deficiencies—that his power might be revealed through your weakness. As my late missionary friend and colleague, Steve Stetler, put it: "God created you as a unique puzzle piece, with a unique space to fill, and if you don't fill it, there will be an empty hole in the puzzle...the portrait will be incomplete."

[Handwritten margin note: 2nd Cor 12:9-11]

[Handwritten note: God's glorified through my weakness because when I admit my weakness He can move in power.]

YOU'LL NEVER KNOW YOURSELF UNTIL YOU KNOW GOD

[Handwritten: Tozer]

As I reflect on those early, very difficult days (especially for me), I see there were misunderstandings about God and myself which were especially problematic; misunderstandings which the Lord used to humble me and to train me. I didn't really understand the nature and character of God. And because I didn't know him, I didn't know myself either.

As I grappled with self-doubt and insecurity, a realization came to me, a realization that if I couldn't do anything else well, I *could* pursue God. I could *seek* him. I could know him. He helped me see that if I would channel all of my doubts, confusion, and nervous energy into a pursuit of him—if I would go deeper into him—he would form me and our work in a way that would glorify him. Though my struggles didn't instantly cease, knowing God became a greater focus.

CHRISTIAN LEADERS ARE CALLED TO A MORE CONTEMPLATIVE LIFE

Allow me to pause for a moment and talk to Christian leaders about choosing a more contemplative life. I always have a tendency to compete *doing* against *being, action* against *contemplation.* And I think one reason is because we don't make enough of contemplation in Christian ministry today. I certainly don't think we make as much of it as the leaders of the early church, who devoted themselves to prayer and the ministry of the word (see Acts 6:1-4).

Following the example of Jesus, the early church prioritized the contemplative life of its overseers. Not contemplation *alone,* but contemplation *first.* They "paid" their elders to pray and to prepare their hearts in the Word of God. They knew that no spiritual movement would be more mighty than its prayers or more sound as its doctrine. Do *we* think this way?

I don't think there are many Christian ministries who would say they pay their pastors and leaders for who they *are* rather than what they *do;* not for *action,* but for *contemplation.* They pay their leaders to set goals, to make phone calls, to write newsletters, to make important decisions, to attend board meetings, to write policy, to settle disputes, to travel and teach, to raise money, etc.—all very important things. But I don't think many leaders are getting paid to spend an hour or two in prayer at the park.

The New Testament church understood that time "wasted" before God was the secret to its peace, its security, its depth, and its breadth. Do we?

The best hope for a weak church today is more Christian leaders who spend time with God. It will produce authority in preaching, vision for ministry, holiness and unity in the body, and joy in fellowship.

If we spiritual leaders and pastors will be honest with ourselves, boredom often plagues us, not because we are not busy, but because we are not contemplative. We have too little passion for what we do because we are not in the presence of Jesus. And let us not deceive ourselves, boredom in the shepherd produces indifference in the flock, and every other sin as well.

Years ago, by the grace of God, I decided to add Acts 6:4 to my job description. Because I am conscientious and want to be a "workman worthy of his wages," I made a conscious decision to count contemplation as part of my workday. I do not feel guilty when I spend hours alone with the Lord each week. In fact, I am far more productive when I spend time with Jesus. I'm a better husband, a better father, and a better leader.

Oswald Chambers said, "Prayer does not fit us for greater work; prayer is the greater work." I have never forgotten this. I truly believe that at the end of our lives, when final results of our life's work have been counted, it will be those things we have done, which we have first heard and seen and decided in the place of prayer and fellowship with Jesus, that will endure.

Little by little, as I learned to walk with God as a young pastor, I began to experience more of the adventure of walking with the Lord, while also walking with our congregation and with my family.

I began conversational walks with the Lord—sometimes in a lovely field nearby, sometimes near the shores of Lake Michigan, and often just walking the streets near our home. On these walks I learned to express my deepest longings to God. I confessed how I wanted to know him and be an effective servant for him. I practiced confession. I confessed to besetting sin and asked for his grace to overcome it. My thoughts were often disjointed. My prayers were often jumbled, chaotic, and probably incoherent. But I was learning to be in an authentic relationship with God.

I read, studied, and memorized Scripture. I listened to a lot of verse-by-verse teaching to help me gain a better understanding of

God's Word. I counseled with men who'd been walking with God much longer than I. I tried to become a better worshiper—with my family and in community with our local church. And during some of my most difficult days the Lord gave me hymns which spoke to me of this God and his love. Many of the hymns I'd sung from childhood became deeply meaningful, like this one by James Grindlay Small:

> I've found a Friend, oh, such a Friend!
> He loved me ere I knew Him;
> He drew me with the cords of love,
> And thus He bound me to Him.
> And round my heart still closely twine
> Those ties which naught can sever,
> For I am His, and He is mine,
> Forever and forever.
>
> I've found a Friend, oh, such a Friend!
> He bled, He died to save me;
> And not alone the gift of life,
> But His own self He gave me.
> Naught that I have my own I call,
> I hold it for the Giver;
> My heart, my strength, my life, my all,
> Are His, and His forever.
>
> I've found a Friend, oh, such a Friend!
> So kind, and true, and tender,
> So wise a Counsellor and Guide,
> So mighty a Defender!
> From Him who loves me now so well,

> What power my soul can sever?
> Shall life or death, or earth or hell?
> No? ==I am His forever.==

I also read from men like A.W. Tozer, who helped me see a more compelling view of God. The God many of us have in our mind is a God too hard to please, but Tozer taught me a God who is "easy to live with":

> Nothing twists and deforms the soul more than a low or unworthy conception of God. Certain sects, such as Pharisees, while they held that God was stern and austere, managed to maintain a fairly high level of external morality; but their righteousness was only outward.... The God of the Pharisee was not an easy God to live with, so his religion became grim and hard and loveless....
>
> How good it would be if we could learn that God is easy to live with. ==He remembers our frame and knows that we are dust.== He may sometimes chasten us, it is true, but even this he does with a smile—the proud, tender smile of a Father who is bursting with pleasure over an imperfect but promising son who is coming every day to look more and more like the One whose child he is. [3]

Do you think of God as bursting with pleasure over you?

The Scriptures paint a beautiful, compelling portrait of God. The most formative portrait in all the Old Testament is found in Exodus 34:6, right after Moses pleads with God to remain with his people. God takes Moses up Mt. Sinai, passes before him, and proclaims himself as,

"The LORD" (Yahweh)

Moses learned that God is "LORD," or *Yahweh,* the God who loves, provides for, defends, and disciplines his people.

"Compassionate"

Yahweh is "compassionate," meaning he genuinely cares about humans like us, and holds toward us a tender attitude of concern and mercy.

"Gracious"

Yahweh is "gracious," meaning he does things for you and me we don't deserve, and goes far beyond what might be expected in order to grant forgiveness and favor.

"Slow to anger"

Yahweh is "slow to anger," meaning he has patience with our failures, including our moral failures, and he's not going to give up on us. *Yahweh* is the God of the second chance!

"Love"

Yahweh declared himself as "abounding" (literally, "great") in "love." The Hebrew word *hesed,* here translated *love* (NIV) or *goodness* (NKJV), is a word used 175 times in the Bible in reference to God. It speaks of his undeserved, unshakable love and kindness. It is a word which speaks of the compassionate, undying, loving devotion of God for people like you and me! However fickle and unreliable we humans may be in our relationship to God, he can be counted on in every situation and at all times to be completely faithful to his promises!

"Truth"

Yahweh is "abounding in truth," meaning whatever he says is correct, reliable, and may be trusted even to the extent of life and death issues, or indeed *eternal* life and death issues.

What a breathtakingly beautiful revelation of God. Is this the God you know? Isn't this the God you want to know?

LOOK FOR GOD IN JESUS

Of all the things God did for me in those years in western Michigan, the most life-transforming was that he began to give me a clearer vision of himself—his perfectly revealed self—*in* and *through* the person of Jesus.

I can hear many of you saying, "I want to know God, but I just don't know where to start!" I understand your confusion. Some of you have grown up with distorted portraits of God. Some of you have grown up with folk theology—beliefs formed without critical thinking or careful, biblical reflection. Some of you have been spiritually abused and find it difficult now to sort out truth from falsehood. I know because I have listened to too many heartbreaking stories.

Some of you find it difficult to see through the many layers of church tradition to the true nature and character of God. Up to this point it's been more about rules than relationship for you. And you wonder, *"What does God really want from me? How does he want me to live my life? What's required for a right relationship with him?"*

Some of you have grown up in godly homes, but you've never taken the time to think through your own faith; you've never put forth the effort to "work out your own salvation with fear and trembling."

You've lived in spiritual complacency far too long. Or perhaps you've compromised with that sin so often that your faith has been wounded. Perhaps your own besetting sin has hidden God's face from you. You want to know him, really know him, but you just don't know where to start.

A beautiful way to begin is to choose God, as the psalmist did: "The sorrows of those who run after another god shall multiply; their drink offerings of blood I will not pour out or take their names on my lips. The LORD is my chosen portion and my cup; you hold my lot" (Psalm 16:4-5).

To choose God as one's portion is to find all satisfaction and enjoyment in him. Not only must I flee *from* sensual pleasures, but I must flee *to* eternal ones. For every weed I pull I must plant a flower. And the empty spaces created by the casting out of counterfeit idols, I must fill with the presence of the good and beautiful God revealed in Jesus.

Now, let's talk about Jesus.

CHAPTER 2

August

A SIMPLE FOCUS ON JESUS

Let's talk about becoming what you behold.

> "From page one to the final word,
> we believe the Bible is a unified story
> that leads to Jesus." — BibleProject

KNOWING GOD AS HE IS FULLY, perfectly, and beautifully revealed in Jesus is the secret to...*everything*. It's that simple!

The desire to know God was something I realized very early in life. Even as I write these words I can vividly recall moments when his presence came near, and the restless, almost wistful desire to know him was strong. These moments were gifts of grace, bought by the intercessions of those who prayed for me.

I see myself as a little boy, staring up at the starry night sky in wonderment, thinking about its mysteries and the God who made such a vast universe.

I see myself, perhaps a little older, traveling with my parents and siblings to our grandparent's home in West Virginia. I stared out the back window at the passing scenery of farms and forests and sky, lost in thought. I remember looking up at bright cloud formations, and at the brilliant colors of the sky at sunset, and thinking what it would be like for Jesus to suddenly appear. I wondered if...hoped I would be ready.

There was a time when as a ten year old I gazed wistfully out the window of our family station wagon as we drove through the winding foothills of Mt. Rainier. The summit on that majestic mountain had been obscured all day by heavy cloud cover, and I was feeling sorely disappointed at not seeing it. Suddenly, the clouds parted, and she burst into view. Her glistening alpine slopes were splendorous and nearly took my breath away. It was a sacred moment for me.

And even in my youth, the wonder of creation was awe-inspiring. Somehow, I knew that the God who created this must be good, but I found it hard to believe that he thought much of me.

But there was another afternoon in that same year, while playing in a field beside our home in Tacoma, Washington, I noticed several 3x5 cards scattered on the ground and picked one up. The shocking, horrifying, even demonic pornographic images I was exposed to in the next few moments would trouble me for several years to come. How I wish now that I'd opened up to my father about this and allowed him to help me process the confusing mixture of revulsion and attraction I experienced; but I felt too embarrassed, ashamed, and guilty to tell anyone.

This discovery, along with occasional exposure to this kind of material throughout my teen years (until I was seventeen), began to wound my conscience and complicate my relationship with God. It was hard to believe that he loved me while I was struggling with secret sin.

I see myself as a teenager, rifle in hand, sitting in a tree stand in the quiet woods, thinking about spiritual things, struggling with the temptations of youth, wishing I could be a better person and that I could know for sure I was in a right relationship with God.

There is yet another scene which plays out very vividly in my mind. In my sixteenth year, my friend Mark taught me to cross country ski. I fell in love with the sport and with the pleasure of sliding silently through snowy fields and woods near our home, now in Greenville, Pennsylvania. That year, my parents gifted me my own skis and boots for Christmas, and late one wintry night, when deep snow covered everything, I slid down Clarksville Street and across Main, through a few side streets, to a large open field sloping upward to a high vantage point overlooking our town. I stood there on my skis in the deep snow for a long time, looking down at empty streets and the shimmering lights of downtown. And in the quiet of the evening my thoughts turned to God. The memory of the deep longing for God in those solitary moments is still with me. I remember praying out loud something like, "God, you know I want to know you and to serve you, but I don't know if I have what it takes right now. Please don't give up on me. Someday I'll get it together." And somehow I felt he was listening and that he loved me, though I couldn't imagine why.

> Somehow, I knew that the God who created this beautiful world must be good, but I found it hard to believe that he thought much of me.

Throughout my difficult teen years these desires to know God never left me, but my life began to feel more and more complicated.

My own wrong, hurtful choices complicated my life and made me feel more and more distant from God. Not only did I hurt myself, but I'm so ashamed of how I hurt others.

Legalism complicated my life, the belief that being right with God depended on my being able to keep his commandments *flawlessly*—which I knew I would never be able to do.

There were times when the rules and traditions of our denomination further complicated my life. Some parts of the religious subculture I grew up in just didn't make sense to me; but I thought God was on *"that side,"* and that if I was ever going to be in a saving relationship with him, I was going to have to be on *"that side"* too.

Why am I giving you these little snapshots of my life? Because I'm quite sure many of you will be able to identify. Your heart is restless for God, but things you've done, things done to you, or ways God has been presented have obscured the true image of God. Is there a way out of this complicated mess? *Yes!*

JESUS IS THAT WAY!

If wrong choices, or religion, or things done to you have distorted your view of God, I recommend Jesus to you. Start with Jesus! Look intensely and steadily at the person and work of Jesus.

The way to God isn't just something Jesus came to show us, but something he is! He didn't come to show us a map of the way to salvation and sanctification, or to point the way... *he, himself,* is the way!

> "And you know *the way* to where I am going." Thomas said to him, "Lord, we do not know where you are going. *How can we know the way?"* Jesus said to him, *"I am the way,* and *the truth,* and *the life.* No one comes to the Father except *through me"* (John 14:4-6, emphasis added).

Philip's question seems to suggest that the way to the Father is somehow distinct from Jesus himself. If I could embellish the conversation which follows, especially with our current context in mind, it might sound something like this:

> "But Jesus, you haven't explained the way to this place where you're going! What exactly do we have to do? What road do we take—the Roman Road? The Gospels Road? The Ephesian Road? The Deeper Life Road? The Surrender Road? The Second Work Road? And what do we say in our prayer? How will we know if we've taken the right way or the wrong way? What words should we use?"
>
> "What!? Philip, we've been together all this time, and you still don't get it? I *am* the way, Philip! Just keep following me. There's no secret passageway. No special formula. No magic words. Simply come with me in complete trust. *Be* with *me*. Love *me*. Look to *me*. Obey *me*. Do what *I* do. Because the way to the Father is... *me!*
>
> "And I didn't come to just speak the truth—I am the truth. I didn't just come to tell you how to find life, *I am the life.* If you have me, Philip, you have the way, the truth, and the life. He who has *the Son of God* has life, and all life is in the Son.
>
> "You're confused, Philip, because you're looking for 'the way' outside of *me*. I am the narrow way. *Salvation* isn't something I *give* you apart from me. Sanctification isn't something I *do* for you apart from me. *I* am all the salvation you will ever need. *I* am all the holiness you will ever need. I in you, Philip, and you in me—here is salvation, here is holiness.

"And by the way, when you choose to come with me, something powerful is going to happen at the center of your being. You're going to become a new person, with a new heart, with a new Spirit indwelling, and a new ability to be, and to do, and to know that you've never experienced before. And I and the Father and the Spirit are going to take up residence in your inner self.

"But all this comes through me, myself! I am not the key to getting something else. I am both the giver and the gift. I am not the secret to some good experience. *I am* the way, the truth, and the life you're looking for. *I am* the way to joy and delight! Me, myself! There is none other.

"I am righteousness. I am comfort. I am power. I am obedience. I am love. I am joy. I am…everything! I didn't come to give you a ladder to God, *I am* the ladder. I didn't come as a shepherd to lead you *to* a door—*I am* the door *and* the Shepherd. By me you will go in and out and find pasture.

"Do you remember when I called you, Philip? I didn't ask you to pray a certain way, but simply said, 'Follow me,' and you did; and your life has never been the same."

The moment we were rescued by Jesus, most of us couldn't have recited the Apostles' Creed, knew little to nothing about the doctrine of justification by faith, and had probably never heard of the theories of the atonement, etc. But we knew we were drowning and were given faith to believe that Jesus could save us somehow. Salvation was not through a doctrinal statement but through Jesus himself, the living doctrine!

Even those who've come into a deeper life of holiness probably have a hard time explaining how it happens, but we do understand that Jesus came to do more than forgive our sins but to make us pure in heart. We opened our hearts to *him* and *he* purified our hearts by faith. *He*—the most important doctrine—*he* does it.

WE MUST MAKE JESUS PREEMINENT ONCE AGAIN IN OUR LIVES AND IN THE CHURCH

The fullness of God dwells in Jesus. He is the image, the visible image of the invisible God, and the image to which we are all being fully restored.

> He is the radiance of the glory of God and the exact imprint of his nature, and he upholds the universe by the word of his power. After making purification for sins, he sat down at the right hand of the Majesty on high" (Hebrews 1:1-3).

Satan's great strategy is to hide God from us. But the work of the Holy Spirit within you is to make Jesus visible in you and then through you.

The entire story of redemptive history leads to Jesus and points back to him. In him we see the radiant splendor of God. In him we see God's holiness, justice, and love fully revealed. We must start with Jesus.

Satan's great strategy is to hide God from us. He hides God with temptation and spiritual compromise. He hides God under layers of tradition and superficial religion. He hides God behind a long list of rules that we cannot keep. He hides him behind clichés and half-truths. He hides him behind an erroneous freedom and a distorted grace. But the work of the Holy Spirit within you is to make Jesus visible in you and then through you.

In every life, the image of God is obscured in some way, but the Holy Spirit wants to reveal Jesus to you.

As a new Christian, then a Bible school student, and then as a young pastor, I went through seasons where misty clouds of doubt obscured the right view of God. Perhaps you can identify. Everybody had an opinion of who God was, and especially, what he demanded of me. And I just didn't know how to make sense of all the voices. Who was right? Who could I trust? I remember praying, "Father, I can't make sense of all these voices and opinions. My tradition teaches one thing, and other traditions teach another. Who is right, God? I want to know the truth! I want to know who you are and what you require!"

As I continued through this season of searching, I began to see that one of the primary reasons God sent Jesus into the world was to make God the Father visible. I had been taught from childhood that Jesus is God, but I hadn't fully grasped that Jesus came to fully *reveal* God to mankind. The Holy Spirit began to reveal certain Scriptures to my heart:

> Whoever has seen me has seen the Father. How can you say, "Show us the Father?" (John 14:9).

> He is the image of the invisible God, the firstborn of all creation (Colossians 1:15).

For in him the whole fullness of deity dwells bodily (Colossians 2:9).

As I meditated on Scripture, I began to see how important Jesus was to my search for God.

START YOUR JOURNEY TO WHOLENESS WITH JESUS

I came to understand that the *fullest* revelation of God is not in his creation, his names, or his attributes. These are wonderful and true revelations. *But the fullest revelation* of God is in the person and work of the Lord Jesus Christ. And every believer who truly grasps and receives this amazing truth will be put on a path of freedom, healing, and wholeness. [1]

In his book, *The Mind of Christ,* Dr. Dennis Kinlaw offers the three laws of Christian discipleship. First, he says, *"find out who Jesus is.* Learn his adequacy for every human need. Then, find out who you are. Realize your inadequacy for serving in God's kingdom, no matter how earnestly you try. And finally, *find the Holy Spirit's power to displace your human weakness with the fullness of Jesus."* What a great word. Start your journey to wholeness with Jesus.

God is a trinity, and yet all that God is in his essential nature, Jesus is. Every attribute of God is an attribute of Jesus. Every name of God is the name of Jesus. Whoever Jesus is, God is. Therefore, any concept of God in my mind inconsistent with the person, redemptive work, and teaching of the Lord Jesus Christ is a distorted God—an idol.

The God of the Old Testament and the God of the New Testament are the same. But only in the gospel can God be fully understood.

As the Lord Jesus became the focal point for me as a young man, the clouds of confusion began to lift. I caught a glimpse of the summit. And with the help of the Holy Spirit, I learned to test the teaching I heard and my own beliefs about God with the question: *Is this teaching and belief consistent with the truth about God which Jesus reveals?*

I became more aware of the beautiful portraits of Jesus in the Gospels. I saw him lovingly ministering to the poor in spirit. I saw his tenderness toward outcasts, his tender touch of lepers, his power over devils, his friendship with sinners, his forgiveness of the guilty, his healing of the sick.

In the Gospels I saw Jesus unhurried and at ease as small children scrambled up onto his lap. I saw his empathy and compassion as he wept with Mary and Martha when Lazarus died, and his demand for holiness and justice as he cleansed the temple. I saw his patience with his prayerless and deserting disciples—men like me. I saw his humble, sacrificial love displayed on the cross. And through Jesus I began to see a clearer picture of God.

A fruitful life and ministry begins by making much of Jesus, but seeing him is not going to be easy. You're going to have to look. You're going to have to give him your full attention. John Piper comments on 2 Corinthians 3:18:

> The Spirit is not working this transformation in us without reference to Jesus. Not while we watch endless hours of empty, trifling TV; not while we dribble our hours away aimlessly exploring the World Wide Web; not while we set our minds on things that ignore Christ. No. The Spirit moves and works and frees in a very definite atmosphere, namely, where we are "beholding as in a mirror the glory of the Lord Jesus" (verse 18). The Spirit exalts

Christ. The Spirit opens the eyes to Christ. The Spirit applies the image of Christ to our soul. If we choose not to focus on Christ, if we go our own way and preoccupy ourselves with other focuses in life, then let us not say, "Where is God?" when we bear the painful fruit of our bondage to sin and experience the law of God as a burden rather than a joy. He has told us the path of freedom. If we spend our days and evenings looking elsewhere, we will probably stay bound up in all our enslavements. [2]

If you want to know God, you're going to have to be more than a weekend warrior. You're going to have to get serious about it!

KNOWING JESUS WILL MAKE YOU BOLD AND COURAGEOUS

And as you get to know God in Jesus, an interesting thing will happen: You're going to become a more bold and courageous Christian. The questions of "who am I?" and "where do I fit?" will begin to be answered. You'll begin to discover your true self.

The world cannot help you at this point, and you certainly won't find answers to your identity by looking within yourself. You must look beyond yourself to the one who knows you better than you know yourself. Too much introspection will lead you to despair, but looking to Jesus will bring transformation.

When you look unto Jesus you will discover your worth. You will learn that you are an image-bearer of God, that through faith in what Jesus has accomplished for you at the cross you are a beloved son or daughter of God, loved with an unshakable love.

The knowledge of yourself in relationship to God will bring immense assurance. It will make you *bold in the things of Jesus and humble in the things of yourself!* ³ You will cease being impressed with clichés and paralyzed by the fear of man. It will put you on the path to authenticity.

Little by little, as you behold the glory of the Lord Jesus, you will be changed into that same image from one degree to the next.

You will become more and more like the God you behold!

IS JESUS PREEMINENT IN YOUR LIFE?

Jesus wants to be "all and *in* all." He wants to be in your worship. He wants to be in your family. He wants to be in your heart and life. He wants to be in your marriage. He wants to be in your work, and in your pleasure.

I'll never forget a conversation I had with my Chinese friend, David S., as he took me back to the airport in Lijiang China. He talked to me of his periodic bouts with debilitating depression, and how the darkness at times becomes so deep that he must close himself into a room for several days, requesting that his wife Jill bring him "simple food." "I read and pray and sleep," he said, "and after two or three days the depression will lift." David continued, and his next words I have never forgotten: "These bouts have been very painful for me, but I would not trade them for anything, because it's during these seasons that *Jesus has become precious to me.*"

Is Jesus this precious to you?

JUST GIVE ME JESUS

New debates and controversies and conspiracies within the church are always arising, sometimes exploding all over social media. It's tempting to dive in. I've found, though, that controversy is smoke in my eyes blinding me from the true vision of Christ and his kingdom.

There is only one cure for a sick life, a sick church, and a sick country. It is not another debate. Not another social media post. It is a deep and abiding love for the God Jesus reveals—love which so captivates us, compels us, constrains us, that we are spoiled for anything else; a "living sacrifice" kind of love which keeps us from being squeezed into the world's mold; an authentic love which also guards us against either heartless traditionalism or the abuse of Christian liberty.

Only love for Christ will hold back the floodwaters of sin and compromise in your life. Only love will compel our children to take up the cross and to lay down their lives for his sake. Only love for Jesus will make us willing to leave father and mother and houses and lands and to suffer hardship for the sake of the gospel.

Voices in my church world have reminded me that God has called us to be a holy, separated people, but that we are "drifting." I agree that the trend towards acceptance of every new fad and fashion is disturbing, that the mindless embracing of broader church methods and philosophy is disturbing, that many Christians are making fast, unprincipled changes in lifestyle and entertainment, that we are becoming mere copycats of the latest trends in music, art, fashion, and entertainment, even in the church, and that we have lost, to a degree, our simplicity, our fervency in prayer, our love for the Scriptures, our spiritual power, and so on. I too am concerned.

The answer is not to preach longer and louder or to isolate ourselves from the world, but to *get back to Jesus.*

Paul's commitment to boast only in the cross (Galatians 6:14) and to know Christ in the power of his death and resurrection (Philippians 3:8-10) protected him from damning preoccupations. He knew that only through the power of Christ's shed blood and victorious resurrection will sin and flesh be conquered. He knew that his soul would only be preserved through faithful obedience motivated and empowered by love. And Paul's commitment to *knowing* Christ and living, dying, and loving as he did kept him from abusing liberty.

The joy in walking in intimate fellowship with the Lord made both legalism and liberalism appear superficial and unsatisfying. The cure for Paul was love. I want this love. We desperately need this love.

The only safe place for you is to cultivate a desire to know Jesus Christ intimately and to share by faith in his death and resurrection. If you'll completely surrender to his lordship, he will fill you with his Spirit and pour out rivers of living water from your innermost being. He will give you *his* love for sinners and imperfect saints. You will share his passion for prayer and his love for the Scriptures. You will become willing to share in his sufferings, for his glory.

Though Count Zinzendorf was of the wealthy ruling class of his day, he was profoundly committed to the Lord. As a young man his life motto was expressed, *"I have one passion: it is Jesus, Jesus only."*

In 1727, twenty-seven-year-old Count Zinzendorf found himself hosting a small community of deeply divided Christian refugees on his large estate in Germany. These refugees came to him from various Christian traditions, including Brethren, Lutheran, Reformed, and Baptists; but being unwilling to lay aside their preferences and traditions, they bickered continually.

Desperate for peace, Zinzendorf went from house to house pleading for unity and finally convinced each family to sign this brotherly covenant: *"In essentials unity, in non-essentials liberty, in all things charity."*

In August of that year during a prayer meeting, the Holy Spirit was poured out on that little group, described as, "the sense of Christ's nearness." This outpouring spawned a one-hundred-year prayer meeting and the sending of hundreds of missionaries around the world. Within a decade or so, one out of three Moravians were missionaries!

What do you think would happen today were we to return Jesus to his preeminent place in our lives and in our churches? Wouldn't this lead to abundant life and peace and joy in the Holy Spirit? *Wouldn't this kind of simplicity lead to revival?*

In conclusion, one of my favorite hymns has become a prayer. I trust that as you reflect on these lyrics, it will become your prayer too:

> I have one deep, supreme desire,
> that I may be like Jesus.
> To this I fervently aspire,
> that I may be like Jesus.
> I want my heart His throne to be,
> so that a watching world may see
> His likeness shining forth in me.
> I want to be like Jesus.

Keep It Simple

He spent His life in doing good;
I want to be like Jesus.
In lowly paths of service trod;
I want to be like Jesus.
He sympathized with hearts distressed,
He spoke the words that cheered and blessed,
He welcomed sinners to His breast.
I want to be like Jesus.

A holy, harmless life He led;
I want to be like Jesus.
The Father's will, His drink and bread;
I want to be like Jesus.
And when at last He comes to die,
"Forgive them, Father," hear Him cry
for those who taunt and crucify.
I want to be like Jesus.

O perfect life of Christ, my Lord!
I want to be like Jesus.
My recompense and my reward,
that I may be like Jesus.
His Spirit fill my hungering soul,
His power all my life control.
My deepest prayer, my highest goal,
that I may be like Jesus.

—T.O. Chisholm

CHAPTER 3

A SIMPLE GOSPEL

Let's talk about
preaching the gospel
to yourself every day.

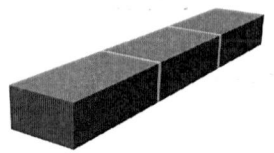

> "Preach the gospel to yourself every day." — Milton Vincent

AS A CHRISTIAN LEADER, you must be utterly convinced that all you will ever be or do is owed to grace alone—to the merits and accomplishments of Jesus. Your motto must be *Jesus plus nothing*. It's that simple.

> And because of him you are in Christ Jesus, who became to us wisdom from God, righteousness and sanctification and redemption, so that, as it is written, "Let the one who boasts, boast in the Lord" (1 Corinthians 1:30-31).

David Yuccaddi, a converted Ifugao tribesman, visited the United States for the first time in 1994. His story had challenged me as a junior in Bible college, and I was eager to meet him. I couldn't explain it, but something drew me to him. Becky and I were pastoring in western Michigan at the time, and took a group from our congregation to a nearby town where David was speaking.

Before inviting David to the podium, a well-respected missionary leader encouraged us with stories of God's power at work in the Filipino church. He spoke of 4 a.m. prayer meetings, of dynamic worship, of evangelistic zeal, and of souls being set free from the bondage of sin. He spoke, too, of David's faith, and of his vision for church planting among the Ifugaos in the highlands of northern Luzon. When David spoke, his message was humble but challenging, and disappointingly brief.

After David's talk, the missionary opened the service for questions. A few were asked and answered, and then a member from our congregation stood up. I'll never forget his question. With a tearful, trembling voice he asked (I'm sure I'm paraphrasing), "What do you think about Christians in America, Rev. Yucaddi? What's going to happen to us? What's God going to do with us? I mean, many of us don't fast as much as you do there in the Philippines. We don't depend on God as you seem to. And we certainly don't pray as much as you do there. What's going to happen to us on the day of judgment? Are we even going to *make it* (to heaven)?"

Such a direct question, I thought. I'm glad I'm not the one having to answer it.

When this brother sat down, the missionary leader, who had been sitting as David fielded questions, suddenly jumped to the microphone. "Now *hold* on a minute," he said to the questioner, his voice rather intense. "Are you *sure* you want David to answer that question? You'd better be *sure* you want the answer because *this man* is going to be honest with you!?"

I began to feel nervous. I wondered what this brother from the Philippines would say. *What has he observed of the American church?*

Is he going to condemn us? Is he going to warn us? Is he going to say that we American Christians probably aren't going to make it to heaven because we aren't spiritual enough? Does he think we're a backslidden people?

David gently waved the missionary aside, stepped up to the microphone, and with calm authority gave the clearest, simplest answer I've ever heard to such a question.

"That's an easy question to answer," he began. "Ephesians 2:8-9 declares, 'For by grace you have been saved through faith, and that not of yourselves; it is the gift of God, not of works lest anyone should boast' (NKJV). We're not saved in the Philippines because we fast, or pray, or anything else," he said, "but because of grace, because we've trusted what Jesus accomplished on the cross of Calvary." And that was it.

What I appreciated then, and still treasure today, is the simplicity and clarity of David's answer. This generation needs such clarity. I've known David as a very close friend and mentor now for nearly thirty years. We've spent countless hours together hiking mountain trails, drinking Nescafe 3 in 1 coffee, discipling new believers, training workers, dedicating new chapels, sharing our hearts, and praying for the coming of God's kingdom. I can tell you that David isn't indifferent to the sins of the church, either in America or in the Philippines. He longs for the sanctification of God's people. But when it comes to the question of eternal life, there is only one way to receive it, and that is through faith in what the Lord Jesus has done for us in the gospel, *period*. Any other gospel is a "different gospel" (Galatians 1:6-9).

The gospel indeed changes us; but even then, we will never be worthy of the grace we've received. Our hope for all eternity rests, not on your own merit or righteousness, but in the merit and righteousness of Jesus. Never forget it. Even on your best day you are only a beggar telling other beggars where to find bread (Matthew 5:3).

In his devotional, *This Day with the Master,* Dennis Kinlaw tells of a young American student who was looking for the church of John Berridge, an English preacher friend of John Wesley. An Anglican pastor showed the young man Berridge's tombstone, where he read this inscription:

> Reader, art thou born again?
> No salvation without a new birth.
> I was born in sin February 1716.
> Remained ignorant of my fallen state until 1730.
> *Lived proudly in faith and works till 1754.*
> Admitted to Everton vicarage 1755.
> *Fled to Jesus alone for refuge 1756.*
> Fell asleep in Christ January 22, 1793 (my emphasis). [1]

Did you notice that after Pastor John Berridge's initial spiritual awakening it took twenty-six years for his faith to find complete *rest* in the finished work of Christ? Sadly, stories like this are not uncommon even among Christian leaders today.

JUSTIFICATION BY FAITH ALONE

The Bible tells us that we are justified by faith. Let's talk about what this *means,* why it is such an urgent teaching today, and why it is safe.

Paul offers a concise version of the gospel in his letter to the Corinthians:

> For I delivered to you as of first importance what I also received: that Christ died for our sins in accordance with the Scriptures, that he was buried, that he was raised on the third day in accordance with the Scriptures (1 Corinthians 15:3-4).

The gospel informs us that we are sinners in need of saving (Acts 4:12); that sin brings separation from a holy God (Isaiah 59:1-2), places sinners under his holy wrath (Ephesians 5:5-6), and results in spiritual and eternal death (Ephesians 2:1; Romans 6:23).

The gospel then informs us that Jesus Christ, the perfect God-man, came into the world *to save sinners* (1 Timothy 1:15). Jesus saves by becoming the Passover Lamb sacrificed in our place (1 Corinthians 5:7), by bearing our sins in his own body on the cross (1 Peter 2:24), by taking the wrath our sins deserve (Isaiah 53:6-7), and by dying, so that through death he might free us from our sins by his blood (Revelation 1:5) and "destroy the one who has the power of death, that is, the devil" (Hebrews 2:14). Jesus saves by being brought back to life by the power of God, so that through faith in him we too are raised to newness of life (2 Corinthians 5:17).

Justification is a legal term which means that a guilty sinner is declared righteous by God on the basis of Christ's death the moment he or she believes. John Wesley said:

> I cannot describe the nature of this faith better than in the words of our own church. "The only instrument of salvation is faith; that is, a sure trust and confidence that God both has and will forgive our sins, that he has accepted us again into his favor, for the merits of Christ's death and passion." (He) accepts

none at all, but by his own free love, His unmerited goodness.

Paul, inspired by the Holy Spirit, and wanting to show the simplicity of justification by faith, made Abraham the chief example (Romans 4:1-25; Galatians 3:6-29; Genesis 15:5-6). Meditation on these passages as a young Christian began to open my eyes to the wonders of grace.

That Abraham and Sarah could have a child in their old age was humanly impossible, even laughable! But in a night vision God led Abraham out of his tent and asked him to "look toward heaven, and number the stars, if you are able to number them" (Genesis 15:5). In my mind I picture a quiet, grassy hillside, a slight breeze blowing across Abraham's face, a brilliant canopy of stars and planets illuminating the night, and Abraham looking up, his face, creased with age, bathed in light.

> As we grow in grace, the Holy Spirit often makes us profoundly aware of our faults. In these moments we must be *humble* enough to confess our faults, and *bold* enough to claim the gracious gift of righteousness offered in the gospel.

"So shall your offspring be," the LORD said (v. 5), and waited for Abraham's response.

I imagine a quiet moment or two passing, and finally Abraham whispering, still looking up, "Okay, LORD, I don't know how you're going to do it, but I trust you." We really don't know what Abraham said, if anything. All we know is what Scripture tells us. In those moments this elderly, *"as good as dead"* (Romans 4:19) friend of God chose not to limit God but simply "believed the LORD, and he counted it to him as righteousness" (v. 6). In that moment the miracle of life was made possible, and future nations were conceived.

Paul says Abraham is the model for all who would be saved. Like Abraham, there's nothing we can do to save ourselves, nothing we can contribute, nothing we can do to produce the life we desperately need. The promise of eternal life is a promise only God can fulfill—a promise he does fulfill simply by our *believing* the gospel.

JUSTIFICATION BY FAITH IS URGENT

The doctrine of justification is urgent because some teaching tends to confuse matters of *justification* and *regeneration* with matters of ongoing sanctification. In sanctification the Holy Spirit is purifying my heart as well as conforming me little by little into the image of Christ (2 Corinthians 3:18). Many of the shortcomings we see in ourselves as we are being sanctified are not matters which can be fixed in a moment but over a lifetime through the renewing of the mind (Romans 12:1-2) and both personal and spiritual discipline (1 Timothy 4:7).

The doctrine of justification is urgent because as we grow in grace, the Holy Spirit often makes us profoundly aware of our faults. In these moments we must be *humble* enough to confess our faults, and *bold* enough to claim the gracious gift of righteousness offered in the gospel. John Wesley made it clear that through the same faith by which sinners are *declared righteous* they are also *kept righteous.* He was an advocate for preaching the gospel to yourself every single day!

He taught that true saving faith is,

Faith in Christ

A full reliance on Christ

Wesley said, "Christian faith is then, not only an assent to the whole Gospel of Christ, but also in full reliance on the blood of Christ; a trust in the merits of his life, death, and resurrection; a (rest in) him as our atonement and our life, *as given for us,* and *living in us....*"

A present faith in Christ

Wesley preached, "By the same faith, we feel the power of Christ every moment resting upon us, whereby alone we are what we are... and without which, notwithstanding all our present holiness, we should be devils the next moment." [2]

BUT WHAT ABOUT SIN?

As a true Christian you will not make light of sin, and you will have power to overcome it; but you are not justified by *not sinning*.

You are not justified by *your* merit, but by the merit of Christ. And don't be surprised when you feel sin clinging to you until you learn to lay it aside (Hebrews 12:1). Sin will not reign in your life, but don't be surprised when you feel the Holy Spirit within you warring against your flesh (Galatians 5:16). This is a common experience every Christian understands. On the last day of 1955, just 10 days before his missionary martyrdom, Jim Elliot wrote about his battle with the flesh:

> A month of temptation. Satan and the flesh have been on me hard on the dreadful old level of breasts and bodies. How God holds my soul in his life and permits one with such wretchedness to continue in his service, I cannot tell. Oh, it has been hard. Betty thinks I have been angry with her, when I have simply had to steel myself to sex life so as not to explode... My unworthiness of her love beats me down. I have been really low inside me struggling and casting myself hourly on Christ for help. [3]

Dietrich Bonhoeffer struggled with feelings of hypocrisy just before his martyrdom as well. Bonhoeffer was a celebrated German pastor, and writer executed by orders of Adolf Hitler. This is one of his last poems from a Nazi prison:

> Who am I? They often tell me,
> I come out of my cell
> Calmly, cheerfully, resolutely,
> Like a lord from his palace.
>
> Who am I? They also tell me,
> I carried the days of misfortune
> Equably, smilingly, proudly,
> like one who is used to winning.
>
> Am I really then what others say of me?
> Or am I only what I know of myself?
> Restless, melancholic, and ill, like a caged bird,
> Struggling for breath, as if hands clasped my throat,
> Hungry for colors, for flowers, for the songs of birds,

Thirsty for friendly words of human kindness,
Shaking with anger at the smallest fate and at the
  smallest sickness,
Trembling for friends at an infinite distance,
Tired and empty at praying, at thinking, at doing,
Drained and ready to say goodbye to it all.

Who am I? This or the other?
Am I one person today and another tomorrow?
Am I both at once? In front of others, a hypocrite,
And to myself a contemptible, fretting weakling?

Who am I? These lonely questions mock me.
Whoever I am, You know me, I am yours, O God. [4]

I have spoken to many believers—some young, some older—who struggle with eternal insecurity because of their battles with the flesh. I understand. The biblical emphasis on true repentance, heart purity, and a conservative lifestyle which I heard as a boy growing up, when not carefully balanced with grace, led some nearly to despair.

While Scripture makes it clear that those who have been born of God do not go on sinning, these same Scriptures do anticipate moments when you will miss the mark (1 John 2:1) and need discipline and reproof (Hebrews 12:5-6). Jesus taught his disciples to pray like this: "And forgive us our *sins,* as we forgive everyone who is indebted to us" (Luke 11:4). As you grow in grace, practice the spiritual disciplines, and learn obedience, you will learn the secrets of victorious living; but there will never be a time in your walk with God that you won't need the atoning blood of Jesus.

While we served in the Philippines, we were visited by an

American pastor and wife. Late one night after we'd tucked the children into bed, this couple shared with Becky and me of the storms they had recently passed through. "So many things were going wrong in our lives, it appeared as though God was actively working against us!" they said. Their finances were hit; the pastor's health was hit; then she became very sick, and their faith took a hit. "Through it all, though," Tonya said, "I learned how much my faith for salvation was built upon how much I did—my performance. Before these weeks of trial, I kind of felt that God *had* to save because I was doing all the right things. I was reading my Bible and praying every day and working hard for him. But when everything was shaken, when I felt myself completely worthless, when I was stripped to *nothing,* I began to see that my salvation was of grace alone." Christ alone is the unshakable, unchangeable foundation.

> As you grow in grace, you will learn the secrets of victorious living; but there will never be a time in your walk with God that you won't need the atoning blood of Jesus.

JUSTIFICATION BY FAITH IS SAFE

Some get nervous when we start talking about justification by faith because it leads some believers to the impression that it doesn't matter how we live. *If we're justified by faith and not by works, do works matter? Won't some take this as a license to sin?* This is a legitimate concern, but what we need is a fuller understanding of the new heart

God gives to those he justifies.

Justification by faith is safe because *with it* God *promises* and *produces newness* of *life*. The biblical word for this newness of life is regeneration (Matthew 19:28; Titus 3:5), and it means a re-birth. Through faith you are "born again," a child of God, possessing his divine nature (2 Peter 1:4).

The Bible also tells us that through faith we are *united* with Jesus Christ. By faith we've participated in his death; our old sinful life died with him on the cross (Romans 6:3). By faith we participated in his resurrection, rising with him to a brand-new life (Romans 6:4, 1 Corinthians 6:9-11). By faith we now participate in his suffering so that in the new Kingdom we will share in his inheritance (Romans 8:17). Think of all this means for you! Think of the potential! Through the cross, sin's power has been broken in your life, and through the miracle of resurrection you have the power to live in a whole new way.

We have been conditioned in our generation to think of salvation only in terms of forgiveness. But forgiveness is not what the full picture of salvation is—not even close.

> For this is the covenant that I will make with the house of Israel after those days, declares the LORD: I will put my law within them, and I will write it on their hearts. And I will be their God, and they shall be my people (Jeremiah 31:33).

> "And I will give you *a new heart,* and *a new spirit* I will put within you. And I will remove the heart of stone from your flesh and give you a heart of flesh. And I will put my Spirit within you, and cause you to walk in my

statutes and be careful to obey my rules" (Ezekiel 36:26-27, emphasis added).

Those God justifies, he also makes new (2 Corinthians 5:17). A new, tender heart means new desires and affections and a new appetite for the Word of God (I Peter 2:2). A new Spirit within means that in salvation Jesus himself, and the Father, come to live in every disciple through the Holy Spirit (John 14:17, 23). The gospel changes one's very nature. Just as my children bear a resemblance to Becky and me because they have our nature, so every true believer will naturally resemble the nature of God. Through faith we've been given a new heart with a newly implanted Spirit.

We can also trust the doctrine of justification because those God justified, he also "glorified" (Romans 8:30). The doctrine of glorification includes the promise that all that has happened to Jesus in his glorious victory over sin and death, and all that has happened in me through the gospel, will completely renew all creation.

The ultimate destiny of the universe is not death and decay but *new creation,* the kind of new creation the sons and daughters of God have already begun to taste through the resurrection: "For the creation waits with eager longing for the revealing of the sons of God... that the creation itself will be set free from its bondage to corruption and obtain the freedom of the glory of the children of God" (Romans 8:19, 21).

The message of Paul in Romans chapter 8 is that just as sinful humans have been released, through the gospel, from bondage to sin leading to death and decay, and have been granted freedom to share in the beautiful, restored image of the God fully revealed in Jesus, so all creation itself will be fully redeemed and restored. The seed of Jesus' body which fell into the ground will not remain alone, but will produce life in me, life in all who believe, and life for *all creation!*

Paul reminds us that the unspeakable suffering I see in me and around me, and the agonizing groans I hear from a dysfunctional earth writhing under a curse, are the labor pains of an old world about to give birth to a brand new one. This is our hope. Heaven is coming to earth.

Our hope is that Jesus took our sins upon himself, nailed them to his cross, and buried them with him in his grave—sins which caused so much dysfunction and misery in our lives.

Our hope is that just as Jesus was raised to a glorious life in a glorious body, free from all decay and corruption, so we have been raised with him, through faith, to a life destined for wholeness and fullness—the fullness we see in Jesus.

Our hope is that when our liberation—our redemption—is complete, all creation will join us, and every son and daughter of God, in full restoration. What has happened to Jesus is happening to us and will happen to the entire universe. *Astounding!*

A dysfunctional world gone forever!

Sin dead forever!

Death and decay gone forever!

Everything and everyone being and doing what they were created to be and do forever!

Here...on earth...the kingdom of God is coming!

This—all of it—is the gospel. It is profound, each part an ocean of truth; but it is simple.

ESTABLISHED IN GRACE

I want you to be rooted in the gospel of Jesus Christ. I want you to be assured that your hope for all eternity is in what he has accomplished *for* you and *in* you. I don't want you to try to serve the Lord out of fear, guilt, or shame. I don't want you to be easily crippled and sidelined by the enemy when you become aware of your own weaknesses and failures. I want you to know what to do when you feel and know that you are inadequate in yourself, even when you struggle with besetting sin. I want you to learn the habit of "preaching" the gospel to yourself every day.

There is a Christian restlessness that we've all known. Am I good enough? Am I doing enough? Are my thoughts pure enough? Do I pray enough? Do I witness enough? Am I sanctified enough? Am I conservative enough? Am I sacrificial enough?

Soul searching is a good thing; but graceless, morbid introspection is not. It makes us fearful, timid, insecure, slavish. Grace is what sets Christianity apart from every world religion. I've been to southwest China several times and watched Tibetan Buddhists spin their prayer wheels, fly their prayer flags, and mumble their mantras, all in a human strain for Nirvana, the Buddhist concept of perfection. But one doesn't have to go to China to see humans striving to make themselves better, to please God, or to live a victorious Christian life. This tendency is everywhere; it's part of our human condition. But we can learn to rest on the finished work of Jesus Christ.

> What has happened to Jesus is happening to us and will happen to the entire universe.

IN SUMMARY

The tragic death of my 24-year-old niece, Shyanne, just a few years ago reminds me of how important it is to get the gospel right. "Shy" had been an angry, foul-mouthed drug addict who had traded in all decency and self-respect to support her addiction. But while spending some months in a Christian rehab center, she experienced forgiveness and complete heart transformation. Our family could hardly believe the change. Only the gospel could have done it. She was redeemed, a new creation with an infectious love for people, a deep hunger for God's Word, and an intense desire to do right. When Shy was killed in a tragic car accident in 2019, she was still struggling with some "stuff," and because of this "stuff," there were some who wondered if she could have made it to heaven.

> The ultimate destiny of the universe is not death and decay but new creation, the kind of new creation the sons and daughters of God have already begun to taste through the resurrection.

Here's what I want you to remember about your salvation:

- Justification is by grace through faith in Christ alone for those who repent both of their sin *and* their moral goodness.

- Those whom God justifies he also sanctifies, transforming one's heart and renewing one's nature.

- Those God justifies and sanctifies, he keeps on sanctifying until one's whole spirit, soul, and body are permeated with the character of Jesus, and until the renewing work of the Spirit heals all our broken places. It'll take time!

- God's indwelling presence through the Holy Spirit is the means and the promise that full transformation will be realized. The Spirit faithfully convicts. He converts. He cleanses. He empowers. He produces the life of Jesus in us. He instructs. He guides. He seals us for the day of redemption. His indwelling presence is the secret to one's desire, understanding, and power. The Holy Spirit makes change happen!

- And finally, the thoroughness to which the life of Jesus penetrates one's total being is in direct relationship to grace-enabled effort. A fruitful harvest of righteousness cannot be *achieved* through human effort and willpower, but it can and must be *cultivated* by our efforts. The penetration of the gospel to every corner of my mind, every secret chamber of my heart, and every act of my body is inseparable from the means of grace I practice, which is where I want to take us next!

CHAPTER 4

A SIMPLE COMMITMENT TO INTEGRITY

Let's talk about
living authentically.

> "The final estimate of men shows that history cares not an iota for the rank or title a man has borne, or the office he has held, but only the quality of his deeds and the character of his mind and heart." — Samuel Logan Brengle

A LIFE LIVED WITH INTEGRITY, and ministries established with integrity, will enjoy the favor of God. It's that simple.

Becky and I moved our family to the Philippines to serve as missionaries in the fall of 1996. The Lord had prepared us for this, and he had clearly opened the door, but we knew immediately we were in over our heads. I was just twenty-seven and Becky twenty-five! We had two small children, just three years of ministry experience, and so much to learn. We waded into those first few months of our assignment, and I desperately sought the Lord for wisdom to know and fulfill his purpose in this new place of ministry.

The churches we were called to serve had a measure of strength. Faithful missionaries had gone before us. The work was blessed with some wise, seasoned, and effective leaders. There was an inspiring culture of evangelism and fervency. A new, younger generation of pastors and "pastoras" was rising and beginning to lead, slowly replacing the pioneer generation. Souls were being saved, and a few daughter churches were being planted by some of the more established congregations. A new and exciting work was beginning among the tribes of northern Luzon, led by a converted Ifugao, David Yucaddi. The well-established Shepherd's College was training and producing men and women for ministry.

But I remember how deeply disappointed we were to learn of some of the broken situations within the organization, even among some of its leaders. We learned of blatant immorality which had never been resolved biblically. We learned of financial mismanagement—sometimes related, I realize now, to a lack of training and accountability rather than to intentional theft. We observed syncretism—the mixing of scriptural truth with pagan custom, of prejudice between tribes, of painful divisions, of a trend toward sensationalism. The problems within the body seemed complicated and tangled. I often wondered if peace and holiness were too much to hope for. And I found it hard to believe that I could bring any new wisdom to the table, or that I, with national leaders, could help form a stronger, more Christlike culture.

And honestly, I was tempted to sweep sin under the rug—to keep quiet because of whom speaking up might "discourage," how it might embarrass the "work," what this might do to our support base, whose reputation might be affected. But as I stumbled through these first harrowing situations, something became crystal clear to me. *I became convinced that integrity would be the key to the favor of God, a favor we desperately needed.*

I became convinced that if we, American and Filipino leaders alike, would commit to *being the people* God wanted us to be, no matter our history, our mistakes, or the complicated situations we faced, he would prosper us! A conviction grew that if we would nurture our families with integrity, preach and teach the gospel with integrity, handle money with integrity, treat the opposite sex with integrity, and communicate with integrity; if we would repent with integrity, by calling ourselves out, by humbling ourselves, by owning our sin; if we would deal lovingly and mercifully but decisively with sin in our churches, then God would begin to mend our broken places.

> He stores up sound wisdom for the upright; he is a shield to those who walk in integrity (Proverbs 2:7).

> Whoever walks in integrity walks securely, but he who makes his ways crooked will be found out (Proverbs 10:9).

These are the people he will bless. *These* will be the vessels of honor, fit for the master's use. Usefulness corresponds to integrity.

So in those early days of missionary life, the matter of integrity caused me to cry out to the Lord. I spent quality time on my face on a coconut polished wood floor in my small office. There I began to understand, in a deeper way, that if integrity would start in us missionaries and church elders, it would spread like a fragrance through the whole of the work; that if we leaders would commit to personal integrity, God would "amen" our commitment for the advancement of his kingdom in the Philippines.

Integrity affects everything we do, especially our preaching and teaching. This powerful word from Dr. Clarence McCartney is imprinted on my mind and returns to me often, especially as I prepare to teach God's Word:

> The better the man, the better the preacher. When he kneels by the bed of the dying or when he mounts the

pulpit stairs, then every self-denial he has made, every Christian forbearance he has shown, every resistance to sin and temptation, will come back to strengthen his arm and give conviction to his voice. Likewise, every evasion of duty, every indulgence of self, every compromise with evil, every unworthy thought, word or deed, will be there at the head of the pulpit stairs to meet the minister on Sunday morning, to take the light from his eyes, the power from his blow, the ring from his voice and the joy from his heart. [1]

Young leader, when you're looking at a mountain of impossibilities—*people* who won't move, *problems* which won't resolve—the best place for you to be is on your face before a God with whom nothing is impossible. And you must stay there until your heart is right and your faith begins to rise, because when that happens, it's going to start spilling over to everyone around you.

Three decades of ministry have convinced me that there is nothing God can't do through people committed to doing life and ministry his way. There's no need to panic or run. If this is where he has *set you down*, then sooner or later the fragrance of Jesus will emanate from you and begin to change the atmosphere. *Believe it! It will happen!*

AN EXAMPLE OF INTEGRITY

As a young missionary, the inspired account of Job helped form my understanding of integrity in profound ways. I took a deep dive into his story.

Job played a number of roles in his day. He was a faithful husband

and God-fearing father, a priest, a businessman, an influential civil leader, and one whose name will be forever associated with suffering. But the key to his lasting influence is *integrity*. His suffering illuminated the grace-sustained integrity of his heart. I began to understand that this dramatic story is not just about *suffering* but what spiritual integrity looks like *through* suffering.

The Hebrew word for integrity, used five times in the story of Job, and only one other time in Proverbs, is *tummah*. It has to do with innocence or wholeness—one whose heart remains undivided or unchanged by trouble.

At the outset of the story we see God commending Job's integrity as Satan strikes blow after blow to destroy it:

> And the LORD said to Satan, "From where have you come?" Satan answered the LORD and said, "From going to and fro on the earth, and from walking up and down on it."

Three decades of ministry have convinced me that there is nothing God can't do through people committed to doing life and ministry his way.

And the LORD said to Satan, "Have you considered my servant Job, that there is none like him on the earth, a blameless and upright man, who fears God and turns away from evil? He still holds fast his *integrity*, although you incited me against him to destroy him without reason" (Job 2:2-3, emphasis added).

Then we see Job's wife mocking him for this integrity,

> Then his wife said to him, "Do you still hold fast your *integrity?* Curse God and die" (Job 2:9).

And his "friends" questioning it,

> Is not your reverence your confidence? And the *integrity* of your ways, your hope? (Job 4:6).

But Job fights for it,

> Far be it from me to say that you are right; till I die I will not put away my *integrity* from me (Job 27:5).

> (Let me be weighed in a just balance, and let God know my *integrity!*) (Job 31:6).

Integrity is important to God, and it must be just as important to us as it was to Job.

A MODEL OF INTEGRITY

From Job, I learned that Christian leaders with integrity are unwavering in their devotion to God despite personal pain and loss. The big life question answered in the book of Job is, "Is there a person of such integrity that they'll stay true no matter the test?" And Job, though flawed in his understanding of God, passes the test.

One can hardly comprehend the waves of grief which fell upon him and his wife in rapid succession, and yet this heartbroken, grief-stricken man never quit on God. Satan lost the bet:

> Then Satan answered the LORD and said, "Skin for skin! All that a man has he will give for his life.
>
> But stretch out your hand and touch his bone and his flesh, and he will curse you to your face" (Job 2:4-5).

I can't help but think of how true Satan's words are in those who lack Job-like integrity like Job's wife. She was right to sorrow. Just imagine what she had lost! It was natural and even healthy for her to grieve. But when grief turns to bitterness, it reflects a lack of spiritual integrity. "Do you still hold fast to your integrity?" she scorned, no doubt implying she was not. "Curse God and die" (Job 2:9).

But look at Job's integrity: "'Shall we receive good from God, and shall we not receive evil?' In all this Job did not sin with his lips" (Job 2:10).

In his commentary, Matthew Henry states: "God speaks of (Job's integrity) with wonder, and pleasure, and something of triumph in the power of his own grace.... *He is the same in adversity that he was in prosperity, and rather better, and more hearty and lively in blessing God than ever.*"

How easy it is to raise our hands and hearts in devotion to the Lord when life is good—when the bills are paid, when we're healthy, when our needs are being met, when our children are thriving, and when our work and ministry is fulfilling. But integrity is proven when the bottom drops out from under us or when we're suffering deprivation. This is what Job taught me. Though he lost everything but God in a few moments—and he thought he'd lost him too—he refused to compromise. This kind of integrity is critical in spiritual leadership.

The maturity of a man may be seen in what he complains about losing. When you look closely at Job's story, you will notice that Job never complains about the loss of his oxen, donkeys, sheep, camels, property, servants, or *even his ten children* whom he deeply loved. Job's consecration was real. He doesn't even complain to his friends about his wife! When his friends came around, this would have been the perfect opportunity to say, "Hey guys, if you had a wife like mine, you'd be depressed too!" But Job never opens his mouth against his wife.

Job's number one complaint had nothing to do with anything material or physical. His greatest complaint was that *he couldn't find God*. He *missed God*. He'd lost the security and assurance which comes from an awareness of God's presence. What an amazing man. What a model for us!

CRITICAL AREAS WHERE INTEGRITY IS NEEDED IN CHRISTIAN LEADERSHIP

As our team of missionaries and national leaders sought to align our lives and ministries with the Word of God, the Lord dealt with us in other critical areas:

Communication

Leaders with integrity communicate with integrity. Jesus taught us: "Let what you say be simply 'Yes' or 'No'; anything more than this comes from evil" (Matthew 5:37). And Peter said, "Whoever desires to love life and see good days, let him keep his tongue from evil and his lips from speaking deceit" (1 Peter 3:10).

There is a refreshing honesty in Job that I also find instructive for spiritual leaders. Job's honesty is a contrast to such deceptiveness: "My lips will not speak falsehood, and my tongue will not utter deceit. Far be it from me to say that you are right; till I die I will not put away my integrity from me" (Job 27:4-5).

People of integrity speak their conscience even when their own reputation is at stake. Men and women of integrity refuse to justify a lie or even bend the truth, even when it is spoken by family members, peers, or people with power. Job's refusal to agree with his friends wasn't because he was proud or couldn't take rebuke, but because agreeing with them would pit him against his own conscience. "I hold fast my righteousness and will not let it go; my heart does not reproach me for any of my days" (Job 27:6).

As we were learning together how to form our lives and ministries in ways God would bless, we saw our temptation to exaggerate our strengths and successes and to minimize our weaknesses and failures. As Christian leaders it's quite easy to present ourselves and our ministries in ways which pull on emotions but which may not be completely honest. We learn to craft words, tell stories, affect voices, portray devotion, and point cameras, not just in creative ways (I love creativity) but in ways which paint embellished, romanticized, and perhaps even in subtle ways, falsified versions of reality. The Lord will not bless this. If we insist on manipulative, human means to achieving spiritual ends, we will never truly experience the power of the Holy Spirit.

Honesty

Leaders with integrity are honest with money and everything else. We steward the resources entrusted to us with honesty and transparency, even the smallest amounts, for, "One who is faithful in a very little is also faithful in much, and one who is dishonest in a very little is also dishonest in much" (Luke 16:10).

I sat in a board meeting some years ago and listened to pastors dismiss the need for financial accountability when people "really trust one another." This just isn't true. When Paul carried a collection of money from congregations in Macedonia to congregations in Jerusalem, he brought men with him who had been approved and appointed by the contributing churches to oversee the money. Why was he so careful?

> "We take this course so that no one should blame us about this generous gift that is being administered by us, for we aim at what is honorable not only in the Lord's sight but also in the sight of men" (2 Corinthians 8:20-21).

This kind of transparency preserves reputations and relationships. As we worked through what integrity would look like for our team in the Philippines, we decided it would mean designating our spending as promised, providing receipts whenever possible, keeping accurate records, and offering a complete and open account of money received and money spent. In this way we would guard ourselves against temptation and suspicion, protect the unity of the church, and preserve our reputation. "A good name is to be chosen rather than great riches, and favor is better than silver or gold" (Proverbs 22:1).

Sexual purity

Leaders with integrity are committed to sexual purity. Perhaps nothing will so test us and refine us as our sexuality. Studies by Barna Group and Covenant Eyes reveal that 68% of churchgoing men and 50% of pastors in the USA view porn on a regular basis, only 13% of self-identified Christian women say they never watch porn, and 57% of pastors say porn addiction is the most damaging issue in their congregation. A big percentage of the research respondents said viewing porn no longer made them feel guilty. [2]

These statistics are startling and depressing, but it doesn't have to be this way. The gospel produces *new affections* and has provided the *sanctification* and *empowerment of the Holy Spirit* to choose right (Ezekiel 36:26-27; 1 Thessalonians 4:3-4). Just listen to Job's commitment:

> I have made a covenant with my eyes; how then could I gaze at a virgin?... Let me be weighed in a just balance, and let God know my integrity! (Job 31:1, 6).

Have you made a covenant with your eyes, too? Purity is no accident! It won't just happen. You'll need Christian community. You'll need to *establish boundaries* in areas where you're weak. You'll probably need to *develop the habit of being vulnerable* and learn to *confess your faults* to another.

I'll never forget how the Lord began to help me to open up and stop trying to battle temptation alone. There was a time early in our ministry when I was seeking God fervently for some specific needs we were facing as a family. I desperately needed fresh grace and perspective. What God did for me during this extended time of focused prayer exceeded those expectations by a long shot.

Toward the end of my sixth day of fasting and prayer, while I was reading a bedtime Bible story to our children, all of a sudden God spoke to my heart in a voice as strong, yet kind, gentle, and inviting as I've ever known. "Son, I want to take you to a new place of freedom," he said, "but I need you to open up about some things." In an instant I knew the things he meant and to whom I must confess. I was stunned, but ready. The things God brought to my mind were not addictions, but God began to show me that there were some strongholds I couldn't break on my own. I needed *another!* I needed the strength of Christian community.

The Bible admonishes us: "Therefore, confess your sins to one another and pray for one another, that you may be healed. The prayer of a righteous person has great power as it is working" (James 5:16). I made up my mind that evening to obey the Word of God, and I did. And it marked the beginning of a new habit of *transparency,* a habit which has provided more grace over these many years than I can even express and has helped me discover deeper and deeper measures of healing. I recommend biblical confession to you.

You'll never reach a time in your life when you're not vulnerable to temptation. You'll need to be watchful. Over these many years of walking with the Lord, the Holy Spirit has become more and more scrupulous with me in this area. My job has necessitated lots of traveling without my wife. I've learned to reach out for prayer when I'm feeling most vulnerable, which is usually after a season of intense ministry. I don't meet with women alone. I don't watch TV (even sports) when I'm alone in a hotel room. There are apps I don't have on my phone. There are stores I don't allow myself to walk into, etc. These are some of the ways I've put boundaries in my life so that I might "discipline my body and keep it under control" (1 Corinthians 9:27).

TREASURE JESUS

I've learned, however, that the greatest protection against the sensuality of our age is to *treasure Jesus* and to *delight in the love of our heavenly Father.* You won't say "no" for long unless you have a more compelling "*yes!*" As a wonderful mentor has said to me: "Sensual pleasures are offered to us as easy substitutes...for the real joy and pleasure we are designed to enjoy as men through the affirm, delight, respect, and the close son-relationship we cultivate with our heavenly Father."

Over the past few years I've developed the habit of praying this beautiful prayer of the psalmist each morning, and I recommend it to you as well:

> Cause me to hear Your lovingkindness in the morning,
> For in You do I trust;
> Cause me to know the way in which I should walk,
> For I lift up my soul to You" (Psalm 143:8).

When I'm hearing deep in my heart the lovingkindness of the Lord, I'm not nearly as vulnerable to forbidden fruit, and neither are you.

PREACHING AND TEACHING

Leaders with integrity handle God's Word carefully. They do their best to present themselves to God as approved workers who have no need to be ashamed, rightly handling the word of truth (2 Timothy 2:15).

Job's "comforters" were abusive, prosperity theology preachers. They taught that good things happen to good people, and bad things happen to bad people, and that if Job were good, the afflictions he was experiencing would not be happening to him (Job 5:17, 22). Preachers like this, who distort the truth, are still around today. Their theology is horribly hurtful and deceitful. Leaders with integrity are careful with how they handle the Word of God.

Years ago, I sat in a conference in Banaue, Philippines, listening as

Filipino pastor, David Yucaddi, taught his pastors on the topic *Integrity in Preaching*. I've never forgotten his main points. "To preach with integrity," David instructed, "means to preach with an understanding mind, a loving heart, a crucified body, and in the power of the Holy Spirit." Indeed, all other preaching lacks integrity. David continued (my paraphrase):

- "We must preach truth we have thoroughly examined and of which we have been thoroughly persuaded."

- "We must always preach truth with love, or we will harden the heart of our hearers, building up their resistance to that which could cure them."

- "And when we preach, we must offer God a purified body; for when we preach with dead desires stirring around in our bodies, our preaching will also be dead."

Such simple yet powerful principles! This kind of preaching will cut the heart and move the will (Luke 24:32; Acts 2:37).

HUMILITY

Leaders with integrity own their faults. No person and no organization is going to be failure free. Mistakes are going to happen, and sooner or later these mistakes are going to hinder progress. You don't have to, but at some point you're probably going to blow it! You're going to say or do the wrong thing, people are going to get hurt, and your reputation will suffer. When this happens, you're going to have to own your faults, humbly, without excuses, and without dragging other people down with you. If you don't, you're going to lose more than you can imagine.

Our family landed in Manila in 2005 after a six-month home assignment. The brother who met us at the airport shared the unspeakably painful news of a moral failure of one of our gifted leaders. And in the months that followed, seven other pastors would fall into some degree of moral sin. After years of spiritual and numerical growth, this would be a year of cleansing and refining and of learning to graciously restore the fallen.

There were many lessons learned during this painful season, but one of the most important was this, that "God resists the proud, but gives grace to the humble" (James 4:6). This unchangeable principle is forever etched in my heart. In every case, those who humbled themselves were little by little restored to blessing; but those who resisted correction, instruction, and accountability could not rise, no matter how hard they tried.

All of us fail in some areas. In 2019 I found myself traveling back to the Philippines to reconcile with a group of pastors with whom my relationship had cooled. These pastors and I each had to own up to our part in the splintered relationship, and by God's grace the result of our honest but respectful sharing with one another has resulted in profound freedom and blessing.

In Job's story, when God comes rushing onto the scene in a whirlwind and confronts him for speaking "words without knowledge," he doesn't run to hide or make excuses. Rather he falls on his face and says, "Behold I am vile; what shall I answer You? I lay my hand on my mouth" (Job 39:3, 4). This is the kind of integrity God blesses.

SUFFERING

Leaders with integrity are faithful to a life of integrity even through seasons of darkness. The thing that made Job's suffering *most* difficult is that it came without explanation; it appeared to be random, or in his words, *"without cause."* He cries out in spiritual loneliness, "Oh, that I knew where I might find him, that I might even come to his seat!" And, "Behold, I go forward, but he is not there, and backward, but I do not perceive him" (Job 23: 8).

Job couldn't see God, feel his presence, or perceive his plan, and this was excruciating. He did in fact express confidence that God knew the way he took, and that when the test was over he would come forth as gold (Job 23:10), yet knowledge of ultimate victory didn't seem to offer much consolation in the process. Serving God in the dark became his greatest test. It will likely be so for us too.

Our son Jesse was born with a rare eye cancer and lost his sight at age four. For some time after his eyes were removed his final request after we'd tucked him into bed at night was, "Daddy, Mommy, please leave the light on!" At first, we declined, telling him that it was bedtime and at bedtime the lights went off. We were also puzzled as to why this was so important to a little boy who was blind. But it was. And in the end, we relented. I marveled as our son, comforted, drifted off to sleep content in the knowledge that though he couldn't see it, he was confident that his room was flooded with light. Why? Because we, his parents, had assured him that it was so.

Job's greatest temptation was that he suffered without the comfort of God's manifest presence. And there will be those times in your life too, times when you have to cling to the promises of God's Word when all is dark. In these difficult seasons God will help you rest in the truth that his light is not diminished even though you can't see it.

INTEGRITY WILL BE YOUR LEGACY

Like Job, you and I can't see behind the scenes of our tests, but future generations will. We, too, are trapped in a limited point of view, but how we respond to every temptation and test really does matter; it matters in heaven, and it matters on earth. Job felt so isolated and ordinary, and he couldn't have imagined the impact his devotion would have upon future sufferers for centuries to come, and neither can we.

One day Jesus joyfully declared while his disciples were out announcing the kingdom of God, just going about their ministry duties, "I saw Satan fall like lightning from Heaven" (Luke 10:18). The disciples didn't see Satan fall, but Jesus did. What encouragement. Imagine it! While you and I are out faithfully doing our sometimes-tiresome work, often blinded to its eternal significance, great victories are being won behind the scenes in the heavenly realm. Integrity matters.

CHAPTER 5

A SIMPLE DISCIPLINE

Let's talk about
getting in the gym.

> "There is a vast difference between training to do something and trying to do something.... Spiritual transformation is not a matter of trying harder but of training wisely." — John Ortberg

TO BE AN EFFECTIVE CHRISTIAN LEADER, you're going to have to get in the gym. It's that simple. Christian maturity, fruitful character, and faithful ministry are gained, not through *earning,* but through *grace enabled effort.*

One of the passages which has helped shape my understanding of the relationship between maturity and effort is from the first letter of Paul to Timothy. He writes, "But reject profane and old wives' fables, and *exercise* yourself toward godliness" (1 Timothy 4:7 emphasis mine).

The word translated "exercise" is the word from which we get our English word *gymnasium.* Exercise suggests tired muscles, heavy lifting, burning lungs, sweat, and other fun stuff! Wesley puts it like this, "Like those who were to contend in the Grecian games, exercise thyself unto godliness. Train thyself up in holiness of heart and life." [1]

What does Paul mean? Does he mean that we can make ourselves godly? Does this mean that we can transform ourselves through self-effort? Certainly not.

Godliness—Christlikeness—can only be produced by the Holy Spirit through faith, but each of us has the responsibility of working *out* what God has worked *in*. Paul teaches us to "*work out* your own salvation with fear and trembling, for it is God who *works in* you, both to will and to work for his good pleasure" (Philippians 2:12-13, emphasis mine). While we cannot produce righteousness any more than a farmer can produce an ear of corn, God gives us the grace to cultivate the field of our hearts for a healthier, holier, more abundant harvest. A deeper spiritual life is both a work of grace and a cooperative effort between you and the Holy Spirit.

DON'T DESPAIR

Satan tempts many Christians to despair because, while they know they've been saved, they wonder why they aren't as patient, humble, or kind as they ought to be, or why they still struggle to completely conquer habits of gossip, anger, worry, fear, slothfulness, impure thoughts, resentment, or the lack of self-control. For too many Christians, there is a wrong expectation that if we've been born again and indwelt by the Holy Spirit, we'll no longer fight these kinds of battles. This is a lie Satan is using to tear away our shield of faith.

While we know that the Holy Spirit can, and does, transform our hearts in instantaneous moments, we also know he brings us to full maturity through processes. The miracles of new birth and Spirit baptism are amazing and take care of the heart problems, but they don't automatically solve all our *character* problems. Be careful of relying on miraculous moments rather than life-long processes.

As E. Stanley Jones put it:

> I believe in miracle, but not too much miracle. For too much miracle would weaken us; would make us too dependent on miracle rather than natural law. Just enough miracle to let us know that he is there, but not too much, lest we should depend on it rather than on our own initiative and on his orderly processes for our development. ²

The reality is that the breaking of old habits of thinking and behaving, the replacement of those habits with healthy ones, and the development of godly character usually requires training. You've got to get to the gym, just as Paul did:

> **A deeper spiritual life is both a work of grace and a cooperative effort between you and the Holy Spirit.**

- To Felix, Paul said, "And herein do *I exercise myself,* to have always a conscience void of offense toward God, and toward men" (Acts 24:16, emphasis mine).

- To the church at Corinth, Paul said, "But *I discipline my body* and keep it under control, lest after preaching to others I myself should be disqualified" (1 Corinthians 9:27, emphasis mine).

- To Titus, Paul wrote, "For the grace of God has appeared, bringing salvation for all people, *training us* to renounce ungodliness and worldly passions, and to live self-controlled, upright, and godly lives in the present age" (Titus 2:11-12, emphasis mine).

The Hebrew writer also speaks of the need for training to share more deeply in the holiness of God: "For the moment all discipline seems painful rather than pleasant, but later it yields the peaceful fruit of righteousness to those who have been *trained* by it" (Hebrews 12:11, emphasis mine).

In the context of wrong desires for the opposite sex, Jesus spoke to his disciples of the need for training. Using hyperbole, he taught that an intensity of zeal and commitment may be required for some to overcome strongholds like lust. "If your right eye causes you to sin," he said, "*tear it out* and *throw it away*. For it is better that you lose one of your members than that your whole body be thrown into hell. And if your right hand causes you to sin, *cut it off* and *throw it away*. For it is better that you lose one of your members than that your whole body go into hell (Matthew 5:29-30, emphasis mine). Of these verses, Oswald Chambers said he had never met a serious Christian who was not "maimed in some way." In other words, Christians serious about holiness will have to deal *seriously* with themselves in those areas where they are prone to weakness.

For some, this will mean taking captive every thought, making yourself vulnerable and accountable to a trusted brother or sister, confessing sin, and forming certain boundaries in your life. It will also mean training your mind and will to resist temptation and to think on good things and developing habits which will cultivate holy affections.

We might wish for a Christian life in which right thoughts, right words, and right behavior were easy and automatic, but such a life has not been offered to us. In his wisdom God has ordained that we are formed into the image of Christ through training.

ALL CHANGE REQUIRES GRACE-FILLED EFFORT

D. A. Carson reminds us that holiness won't happen without effort with these incredibly pointed words:

> People do not drift toward holiness. Apart from grace-driven effort, people do not gravitate toward godliness, prayer, obedience to Scripture, faith, and delight in the Lord. We drift toward compromise and call it tolerance; we drift toward disobedience and call it freedom; we drift toward superstition and call it faith. We cherish the loud indiscipline of lost self-control and call it relaxation; we slouch toward prayerlessness and delude ourselves into thinking we have escaped legalism; we slide toward godlessness and convince ourselves we have been liberated. [3]

How convicting!

ALL CHANGE ALSO REQUIRES A CHANGE OF MIND, WHICH ALSO REQUIRES TRAINING

The first thing you've got to exercise is your *mind*. Your mind is the real battlefield—the territory where battles are either won or lost. Until we learn to think differently, we cannot experience lasting change (Romans 12:2). As your mind is sanctified by the Word of God, you'll begin to experience a difference in your affections and desires. As your affections and desires are sanctified, your behavior will be sanctified as well. A sanctified thought leads to a sanctified desire, which leads to a sanctified act. We cannot reverse this order. The attempt of behavior change without a change of mind and affections will prove a fruitless effort.

IT'S NOT UNCOMMON TO STRUGGLE

I want to emphasize again that just because you are struggling in certain areas of your Christian walk doesn't mean that your commitment to the Lord isn't real, or that you're more broken than other people. Not at all. If you're a believer, you've been set free at the cross. His Holy Spirit indwells you. You have the divine nature and all you will ever need for life and godliness. But you need to get serious about training. You need to work on some spiritual and personal disciplines. And these disciplines or habits will determine the kind of person you become.

If you tend toward overindulgence (who doesn't?), get in the gym and exercise self-control until saying "no" to yourself becomes easier and your habits begin to change. Maybe you're a procrastinator. Okay, confess that to the Lord, ask him for strength, and then commit yourself to do the hard things *first*. Does your mind wander to places it shouldn't? This is a common problem for Christians, but through the Holy Spirit you must work hard to capture those thoughts and make them obedient to the Lord Jesus Christ.

EXERCISE IS NECESSARY BECAUSE HABITS HAVE BECOME ENTRENCHED IN YOUR CHARACTER

I recently watched a documentary series on the World War II battle of Iwo Jima. This historic battle involved 110,000 American soldiers, nine months of heavy bombardment before landing (hardly an inch of the island had been untouched by the bombings) from sea and air, and still the USA suffered over 24,000 casualties, including over 6,000 deaths, in just five weeks. What was the cause of so much bloodshed? The Japanese imperial army had dug 11 miles of tunnels and was well hidden and protected under layers of volcanic rock, and getting to them required another strategy.

> Many of the things wrong with us and broken in us are hidden even from ourselves, so we must put ourselves continually before God so he can reveal them and so we can put them to death.

The Japanese army's remaining 25,000 soldiers could not be taken out from the sea or air, but had to be burned out, shot out, taken out systematically, at close range, one cave at a time. This horrible battle became one of the bloodiest of the entire war.

In the same way, I think the invisible enemies entrenched within each mind and heart demand a revelation of ourselves by the Holy Spirit, and his specific, systematic, close-range application of the Word of God to our hearts. General surrender to God won't sanctify us in many of the ways we need to be sanctified. Many of the things wrong with us and broken in us are hidden even from ourselves, so we must put ourselves continually before God so he can reveal them and so we can put them to death (Colossians 3:5-10).

I have a friend whom God has powerfully transformed and healed of a painful, self-inflicted spiritual wound, and yet there are areas of ongoing struggle. He called me one day and said, "I believe that God is closing every other door for me during this season of my life so that I can learn the discipline of perseverance. My life up to this point has been a series of *unfinished projects,* and I know that if I am ever going to truly succeed in my relationship with God, I'm going to have to learn to finish what I start. My impatience is a character issue that affects every other area of my life!" I was amazed by my friend's humility and insight. Today, he's growing deeper and stronger—through effort.

EVEN THE DEVELOPMENT OF CHRISTIAN VIRTUES AND THE FRUIT OF THE SPIRIT REQUIRES EFFORT

The apostle Peter reminds his readers that while God's power has given them everything having to do with life and godliness, so that they might share in the divine nature, they still have a lot of good work ahead:

> For this very reason, *make every effort* to supplement your faith with virtue, and virtue with knowledge, and

knowledge with self-control, and self-control with steadfastness, and steadfastness with godliness, and godliness with brotherly affection, and brotherly affection with love. For if these qualities are yours *and are increasing,* they keep you from being ineffective or unfruitful in the knowledge of our Lord Jesus Christ (2 Peter 1:3-8, emphasis mine).

See here how *nature* and *nurture* come together? Peter assures us that while the divine nature is from God, the full operation of his nature within us requires effort. In the original language his admonition to "give every effort" is very emphatic. He makes it very clear that building spiritual virtue on the foundation of saving faith isn't going to be easy. We must *be fully engaged and in total earnest* to nurture and cultivate the divine nature which has been planted within us.

Sometime ago, Becky and I had been meditating on the need to cultivate gentleness in our interactions with one another and our children when we came across this teaching found in Lettie Cowman's devotional, *Streams in the Desert:*

> The graces of the Spirit [like gentleness] do not settle themselves down upon us by chance; and if we do not discern certain states of grace, and choose them, and in our thoughts nourish them, they will never become fastened in our nature or behavior. Every advance step in grace must be preceded by first apprehending it, and then prayerful resolve to have it. [4]

Practicing virtue until it is "*fastened* in our nature and behavior"? How often do I think like this?

Becky and I have hosted a couples Bible study in our home for a number of years. During one fellowship, a young mother expressed her frustrating inability to live a consistent Christian life. "This probably sounds really dumb," she exclaimed, "but the thought has sometimes crossed my mind that perhaps I'm just not one of God's chosen, that maybe I'll never be strong no matter how hard I try!"

I think there are many sincere believers who deeply wonder if the highest levels of devotion to God are reserved for "special" Christians. But God is no respecter of persons. Our problem is often simply a lack of character strengthened through constant practice.

The divine nature, through the Holy Spirit, is the source of *love;* but the act of loving all people even while they are acting toward us in unlovable ways requires training.

The divine seed of gentleness is planted in our hearts by faith, but gentle responses to harsh accusations and gentle answers to quarrelsome individuals are achieved through the training of the tongue.

The Holy Spirit is the source of peace, but learning to keep our hearts in perfect peace amid tense and stressful circumstances requires the training of the soul.

Self-control

Self-control is also the fruit of the Holy Spirit; but temperance in our emotions and appetites requires the practice of self-discipline, especially for those who aren't used to saying "no!" to themselves.

Patience

This virtue is also planted in our souls from God. It is a quality of the divine nature. But the ability to wait for that which we long for, to delay pleasure, and to be still will only be fastened in our character through intentional effort.

Faithfulness

Faithfulness is a characteristic of the divine nature, but being on time, working hard, keeping our word, and following through on our commitments require vigilant training, especially for those who are prone to laziness.

Humility

Humility is of the Holy Spirit, but considering others better than we are requires training.

Heart purity

Heart purity is also from the Holy Spirit by faith, but the habit of guarding our heart is gained through diligent spiritual exercise.

Joy

Joy is a fruit of the Spirit, but learning to praise the Lord at all times is a trained choice of the will.

Through redemption God gives us all the building materials we will ever need for godly character, but the building of that character, stone by stone, room by room is our daily challenge. Where does grace fit in? Grace is what believers experience when they are busy with training.

WHAT DOES TRAINING LOOK LIKE?

What are some of the specific training exercises that will help you grow in character? It will help us to divide these into two categories: spiritual disciplines and personal disciplines.

Training involves the spiritual disciplines.
Spiritual disciplines train us. The spiritual disciplines are a means of grace. Through the exercise of these disciplines, the Holy Spirit will free us from the tyranny of self, appetite, materialism, and pride, and bring healing to our souls, forming us into the image of Jesus.

> The discipline of solitude is spending time alone with God (Luke 5:16).
>
> The discipline of meditation is talking to ourselves about the Word of God (Psalm 1:2).
>
> The discipline of fasting and self-denial involves skipping meal(s), exercising moderation, or denying ourselves certain pleasures for a time to seek the face of God (Daniel 9:3, 22-23).
>
> The discipline of simplicity involves learning to live with less to focus on the most important things (Matthew 6:33).
>
> The discipline of sacrifice involves giving our time and resources beyond what seems humanly reasonable to cultivate a greater dependence on God (Mark 12:43).
>
> The discipline of private prayer involves adoration, petition, confession, and thanksgiving (Matthew 6:6-15).
>
> The discipline of service involves the exercise of our spiritual gift(s) for the edification of our local church (Luke 22:25-26).

The discipline of worship is the offering of uninhibited praise and adoration to God (Psalm 103:1).

The discipline of Christian fellowship involves the meeting with other Christians for the purpose of edification (Acts 2:42).

The discipline of confession involves the humbling of myself before God and a trusted Christian friend (James 5:16).

The discipline of submission involves the voluntary placing of myself under the authority of another (1 Peter 5:5).

Exercise involves personal discipline.
Self-renunciation or self-mortification trains us. Self-renunciation has to do with one's commitment to saying a decisive "no" to physical appetites when they become too strong, and especially when they begin to erode one's spiritual life. Paul said it like this: "And everyone who competes for the prize is temperate in all things.... But *I discipline my body* and keep it under control, lest after preaching to others I myself should be disqualified" (1 Corinthians 9:25, 27, emphasis mine).

There are at least five *personal disciplines* you must work on:

The discipline of our thought life involves taking every thought captive to obey Jesus (2 Corinthians 10:5).

The discipline of our appetite involves temperance in all things (1 Corinthians 9:25).

The discipline of our tongue involves the mastery of whole bodies through the mastery of our words (James 3:2).

The discipline of our temperament involves the ruling of our own spirit (Proverbs 16:32).

The discipline of our time involves training ourselves to pursue things that are excellent and to glorify God in all things (Philippians 1:9-10; Colossians 3:17; 1 Corinthians 10:31).

These spiritual and personal disciplines, along with chastening (Hebrews 12:11), are the primary training exercises which allow God's grace to flow in our lives. These will help us keep natural desire in check, produce good habits, and allow the Holy Spirit to reign as he wants to and to bring us into conformity to Jesus Christ.

AN EXAMPLE OF PERSONAL AND SPIRITUAL DISCIPLINE

Daniel was likely just a teenager when the Babylonian army attacked Jerusalem and carried him and his friends off to Babylon. I can imagine the sad scene as Babylonian soldiers break into Daniel's family home, bind him in shackles, and lead him away. No doubt there were pleas and tears from God-fearing parents and friends; but as the walls of Jerusalem disappear behind him, I can see Daniel wiping his eyes and saying in his heart, "The Babylonians can take me out of Jerusalem, but they'll never take Jerusalem out of me!"

Upon arrival in Babylon, Daniel and his friends were slammed with everything Babylonian—culture, language, literature, cuisine. They were even given Babylonian names. All this should be understood as an intentional effort to change their whole identity.

And what I love about Daniel is that he wasn't afraid to engage Babylon. He possessed a flexible, generous, likable spirit. He engaged the culture, learned the language, excelled in "Babylon University," and graciously tolerated the name change. He never came across as preachy or judgmental or rude, and because of this, God gave him much favor. But Daniel was not stupid. He knew the danger of allowing Babylon to squeeze him into its mold, so he established some unique habits (customs) to guard his heart and preserve his identity.

> But Daniel resolved that he would not defile himself with the king's food, or with the wine that he drank. Therefore he asked the chief of the eunuchs to allow him not to defile himself (Daniel 1:8).

> Now when Daniel knew that the writing was signed, he went home. And in his upper room, with his windows open toward Jerusalem, he knelt down on his knees three times that day, and prayed and gave thanks before his God, as was his custom since early days (Daniel 6:9-10, NKJV).

"But Daniel resolved...." Daniel resolved to practice some disciplines (customs) which would serve his desire for spiritual excellence.

Daniel's vegetarian food fast wasn't just about the food, but about association and about identification. Some of the food wasn't kosher, and some would have been offered to Babylonian idols. These facts would have put some foods off limits for Daniel, but there was more to it than this, "for the king's opulent dinners would include a spirit of self-indulgence and an atmosphere of idleness, leisure, and intoxicating pleasure." [5] By guarding his diet, Daniel was fleeing self-indulgence.

The open window facing Jerusalem wasn't just about prayer, but a custom he established to preserve his heart. Daniel could have prayed privately with the windows closed, but I think he threw open the window and faced Jerusalem because, 1) facing Jerusalem was a visual aid helping to preserve his love for his people and his God, 2) he would *not* be driven by fear, 3) he wanted to keep a clear testimony, and, 4) by defying the natural desire to protect and promote himself, Daniel placed himself in the hands of God. Daniel's actions said in essence: *"God, I know that protection and promotion come from you alone. I don't need to be afraid."*

The morning, noon, and night prayers weren't about compulsory habits, but about cultivating ceaseless hope in God's promise of a coming Messiah who would establish his kingdom.

In my imagination, I see Daniel's nephew watching him practice his daily routines; and perhaps one day he even stated, "Hey Uncle Daniel, when I grow up, I'm not going to do the vegetarian diet, or the open window, or the prayer facing Jerusalem, or three times a day prayer stuff that you do, because it's not in the Bible."

And I can hear the wise uncle gently responding, "Come over here young man and look out this window. What do you see?"

"I see the lights of Babylon, Uncle!"

"That's right, son. We're surrounded by Babylon. And over that distant horizon, beyond the reach of your vision, there is a city of which you've heard but have not yet seen. It's the city of our birth. It's our true home. It's the city of God. It's our inheritance. It's where, according to God's promise, we'll return someday if we keep her in our hearts."

"Nephew, you may not choose to accept all *my* disciplines. But I want to ask you, 'What decisions are you going to make to help you preserve your heart for Jerusalem? What habits will you form to keep Babylon from encroaching on your heart and stealing your vision of our homeland? Someday, God is going to fulfill his promise; and those who haven't lost their affection for Jerusalem and Jerusalem's God—who haven't become rooted in *this* city—will return there with singing and laughter. Babylon will crumble. Babylon will fall. Jerusalem is established by God and will endure forever!"

Every successful Christian follows Daniel's example in some way. Successful men and women train themselves, not to earn God's favor or to follow a man-made list of rules, but to preserve our love for Jesus and to become all he wants us to be. Daniel established convictions which, in *his* time, *his* world, and in *his* generation, helped preserve his heart. We must do the same.

IN CONCLUSION

As we wrap up this chapter, it may be helpful to some to offer two cautions. First, be careful of thinking that to be holy you'll need to *isolate* yourself from the world. In Daniel's case, we see that while God didn't want his people to lose their identity and adopt pagan ways, he did intend for them to bear fruit, even in exile, and to seek the good of whatever country they found themselves in.

A second caution is to beware of legalism. Just as Daniel didn't practice certain disciplines just because others were, neither should we. George Muller warned of this kind of behavior:

> I have often remarked the injurious effects of doing

things because others did them, or because it was the custom, or because they were persuaded into acts of outward self-denial, or giving up things (while) the heart did not go along with it, and (while) the outward act was not the result of the inward powerful working of the Holy (Spirit), and the happy entering into our fellowship with the Father and with the Son.

Everything that is a mere form, a mere habit and custom...is to be dreaded exceedingly.... Things should not result from without, but from within. The sort of clothes I wear, the kind of house I live in...all such like things should not result from other persons doing so and so, or because it is customary among those brethren with whom I associate to live in such and such a simple, inexpensive, self-denying way; but whatever be done in these things, in the way of giving up, or self-denial, or deadness to the world, should result from the joy we have in God, from the knowledge of our being the children of God, from the entering into the preciousness of our future inheritance, etc. [6]

You must train yourself toward godliness!

CHAPTER 6

A SIMPLE HUMILITY

Let's talk about
getting over ourselves.

"There is a soul, none half so beautiful, as a common, unpoetic life." — Dr. Bill Ury, speaking on the life of Jesus' earthly father, Joseph

"All God's giants have been weak men who did great things for God because they reckoned on God being with them." — J. Hudson Taylor

YOU NEED TO GET OUT OF YOUR OWN WAY. It's that simple.

> The fear of the Lord is instruction in wisdom, and humility comes before honor. (Proverbs 15:33).

Of all the truths the Lord has been teaching me over these 26 years, none is more important than this, that "God *opposes* the proud but *gives grace* to the humble" (James 4:6, emphasis mine). You might want to read that again and give it some serious thought. I think James wants us to imagine our lives and ministries as a battlefield where God is giving all grace—fighting our battles and leading us to victory—up to the point where we refuse to face ourselves. At *that* point, God will *turn* and begin to *oppose us*. What a *terrifying* thought! God sometimes leaves us just defenseless enough to feel the pain of Satan's fiery arrows, cuts off escape routes until we confess our faults, and lets us struggle until we fully submit to his Word. If this thought *doesn't* terrify you, you may not fear God as you should.

This truth has instructed me many times when I have hit a wall, when I've been under the "mighty hand of God" (1 Peter 5:6), when I know I've failed but am having a hard time admitting it. I have come to realize that no matter how hard it is at the time to do so, if I'll humble myself, God's blessing will be restored to me. I've also learned that making excuses and resisting correction is a waste of time. I might as well go ahead and *get it over with,* because God is *relentless* in his pursuit of holiness in me! He's not known to give way.

I'll never forget how I found myself struggling as a missionary. There were problems; and hardly noticing, I began to react in impatient, un-Christlike ways. It was difficult for me to admit that I might be part of the problem until one morning in my quiet time I sensed the Lord speaking to my heart. The conversation went something like this:

God: "Son, you're angry, and you're operating out of anger."
Me, in defense mode: "I'm not angry, Lord, I'm a *missionary.*"
God, unimpressed: "Well, son, you're an *angry* missionary!"

I remember laughing out loud at the thought that my cover had been blown. Being a missionary was giving me a false sense of superiority and spirituality. I was hiding from the truth about myself behind my missionary status, as if being a missionary made me a super saint who was above correction. Acceptance of the Spirit's conviction became yet another pivotal moment in my journey. There have been many more!

Pride is enemy number one for the Christian leader. It will always be your greatest problem, your greatest cause of defeat...*until you die to yourself.* While in Africa a few years ago, I heard a preacher tell a funny story about a man who walked around with meat in pockets, but wondered why the village dogs wouldn't leave him alone. He never connected the meat in his pocket to the growling, barking, biting dogs. What a vivid picture of pride. Pride is the meat in our spiritual pockets, attracting every form of temptation and leaving us wounded and defeated, until we empty our pockets at the foot of the cross.

What does pride, the "meat in our pockets," look like? Pride wears many disguises, but they all have to do with *self*.

Pride looks like self-righteousness, which is not only a sense of moral superiority to others, but a striving to be righteous and good on my own. This self-righteous tendency is familiar to all of us. In his Sermon on the Mount, Jesus taught that the path to spiritual prosperity is by way of spiritual bankruptcy: "Blessed are the poor in spirit," he said, "for theirs is the kingdom of heaven" (Matthew 5:3). No one made aware of their own poverty will think themselves superior to others.

> **Pride is enemy number one for the Christian leader. It will always be your greatest problem, your greatest cause of defeat…until you die to yourself.**

The word Jesus used for "poor" in this sermon literally means *beggarly* poor, or *utter bankruptcy.*

I see many beggars as I travel around the world, and I can tell you that spiritual and human beggars have much in common. Most beggars outside the west have been driven to this dehumanizing existence by desperation. They are among the displaced. They are among the refugees. They are the elderly, the widowed, the blind, the crippled, the unemployable. Abject poverty has driven them to an undignified position—to holding out an empty hand appealing to the kindness and pity of strangers. According to Jesus, an awareness that this is our condition, in the spiritual sense, is the kind of spirit God is looking for in disciples. This kind of poverty is sure to receive the favor of God.

Have you come to the place where you know you could never merit salvation? Are you convinced that you'll never be able to overcome your besetting sin apart from the Spirit of God? Do you know that you are truly destitute on your own, and that all you will ever be or do is a credit to grace? Can you sing these lyrics, written by Edward Mote, from your heart?

> My hope is built on nothing less
> Than Jesus' blood and righteousness;
> I dare not trust the sweetest frame,
> But wholly lean on Jesus' name
>
> On Christ, the solid rock, I stand:
> All other ground is sinking sand;
> All other ground is sinking sand.

You will continue to struggle in your spiritual life and in Christian leadership until you recognize your poor, beggarly condition apart from grace.

I love the story of the obnoxious blind man who sat by the road as Jesus and a large crowd passed by. [1] *"Have mercy on me!"* he shouted. People were irritated and perhaps even embarrassed by his unrestrained shouting, but their angry rebukes couldn't silence him. "But he cried out all the more." Why? Because he knew Jesus was his only hope for sight! *How foolish would it have been for him to cling to his dignity but remain blind!?* There is a real sense in which every person who has received healing *from* Jesus or dispensed the healing *of* Jesus to others has become as poor in spirit as this blind man.

But pride has many other faces too.

Pride looks like self-fulfillment, the search for personal happiness apart from God.

Pride looks like self-gratification, the choice to gratify the desires of the flesh rather than the desires of the Spirit.

Pride looks like self-promotion, the seeking of human honor above the honor of God.

Pride looks like self-sufficiency, the tendency to trust ourselves rather than God.

Pride looks like self-pity, the giving in to the feeling that we deserve better than we're getting.

Pride looks like self-preservation, seeking what *we* believe is best for our lives rather than abandoning ourselves to the wise and beautiful plan of God.

Pride looks like self-will, choosing my will rather than submitting to God's authority and the authority structures he has placed around me.

All of these "selves" must go if you would be a successful Christian and leader!

JESUS MODELS HUMILITY

Against the backdrop of pride, we see the self-denying, self-giving, self-sacrificing life of Jesus, and learn that his way of thinking and living is not only *possible* but *expected!* I urge you to read the following words slowly and thoughtfully:

> Do nothing from selfish ambition or conceit, but in humility count others more significant than yourselves. Let each of you look not only to his own interests, but also to the interests of others.
>
> Have this mind among yourselves, which is yours in Christ Jesus, who, though he was in the form of God, did not count equality with God a thing to be grasped, but emptied himself, by taking the form of a servant, being born in the likeness of men. And being found in human form, he humbled himself by becoming obedient to the point of death, even death on a cross (Philippians 2:3-8).

With these profound words Paul tells us that Christ existed in the *"form of God"*—the same essence and nature of God, and that he was God's equal in every sense. Jesus is the *"express image"* of God—his exact representation—the perfect stamp of his nature and essence (Hebrews 1:3). Jesus is the invisible God made visible (Col.1:15; Philippians 2:9), the creator and sustainer of everything, upholding all things by his power (Col. 1:16-17), and yet he entered this broken world as a *servant!* And he's inviting you to be like him.

Jesus "emptied himself," a phrase which comes from the Greek word "kenosis," which means *to make empty or lay aside.* Jesus Christ was and is *truly* and *fully* God, deserving of all the rights and privileges of his deity; yet he never considered equality with God as wealth to be hoarded, but invested for the sake of love. Though his divine nature could never be laid aside, for the sake of *redemption* he laid aside all distinction and honor and *reputation,* to become *weak,* to appear *common, ordinary,* and *under-privileged.* "Though he remained full (John. 1:14), yet he appeared as if he had been empty; for he veiled his fullness from the sight of men and angels." [2] Herein is our truest revelation of humility and our holy example to follow.

Consider for a moment the privileges Jesus laid aside during his earthly ministry compared to the privileges every Christian leader has at some point been tempted to seek:

> Jesus laid aside heavenly glory (John 17:5), while we too often seek after glory, demand recognition, clamor for titles, and make a name for ourselves.

> Jesus let go of his reputation, while we demand respect, afraid to become *less,* that Jesus might become *more* (John 3:30).

> Jesus laid aside eternal riches (2 Corinthians 8:9), while we covet wealth.

As I contemplate what our Lord laid aside, I am forced to see the foolishness of the things I've clung to as "my" rights. I need the mind of Jesus, and so do you.

Paul goes on to say that Jesus became as a slave to the will of his Father, by taking the form of a servant; a slave without rights or reputation, whose entire life was consumed with doing what pleased the master.

When Jesus entered the ministry, he *surrendered* his will to the will of his Father and chose a life of *humble dependency.* He did not think in terms of personal reputation or what he would gain. He knew that his calling was to take care of the things that mattered to the Father, and that the Father would care for the things that mattered to him.

Let *this* mind be in *you!*

Jesus shared the sufferings of those he came to save—"being born in the likeness of men. And being found in human form..." Jesus was more than God in a body, but took on all the essential attributes of humanity. He became fully man, teaching us that the one who thinks like Jesus has a willingness to *share* in poverty, hunger, thirst, homelessness, weariness, sadness, physical and emotional pain, and even betrayal for the sake of destroying Satan's kingdom and building God's kingdom. Hear these words:

> Since therefore the children share in flesh and blood, he himself likewise partook of the same things, that through death he might destroy the one who has the power of death, that is, the devil (Hebrews 2:14).

> Therefore he had to be made like his brothers in every respect, so that he might become a merciful and faithful high priest in the service of God, to make propitiation for the sins of the people (Hebrews 2:17).

Let *this* mind be in *you!*

Lastly, Paul says Jesus "humbled himself by becoming obedient to the point of death, even death on a cross." The humility of Jesus was most evident in his persistent, determined obedience to the Father's will *even when it meant death on a cruel Roman cross.*

Speaking of obedience, when my son, Timothy, was just a little boy, I said to him one day, "Son, Dad's going to be gone for a couple of hours, and while I'm away I want you to clean up your room for Mommy."

"Okay, Daddy!" he said cheerfully. When I returned, he met me in the kitchen with a big smile on his face. *"Look, Daddy!"* he said, proudly looking around at an empty sink and clean countertops. "I washed *all* the dishes and...!"

"Oh, that's *really* good," I said, following his gaze. "And did you clean your room, *too?*" I asked hopefully. His head fell and the smile vanished. "Uh...no daddy."

"Then you know the consequence of disobedience," I said sadly. I punished my son because he chose his own path of obedience, rendering his service nothing more than a self-pleasing act. Others may have applauded his industry, but I knew better, because even the most heroic perseverance in our own selfish pursuits is what the Bible calls rebellion. A humble disciple will show his love for God by doing the very thing, at the very time, in the very place God has instructed.

> A humble disciple will show his love for God by doing the very thing, at the very time, in the very place God has instructed.

This is what Jesus did.

And Jesus did not retreat even when he knew obedience would cost him everything. He did not stray from the path of obedience even when it meant betrayal, loneliness, denial, false accusations, cruel torture, social rejection, humiliation, and death. Amazingly, the nearer he got to the moment of crucifixion, the more he *determined* to go through with it (Isaiah 50:7). And through the whole cross ordeal, the Holy Spirit enabled Jesus to learn obedience through the things he suffered (Hebrews 5:8) and to keep silent when he was slandered (Isaiah 53:7), "entrusting himself to him who judges justly." In this he has left us "an example," so that we might "follow in his steps" (1 Peter 2:21-23).

Let *this* mind be in *you!*

PRIDE IS A THREAT TO SUCCESS

Pride must be dealt with because it is undoubtedly the cause of much attrition among Christian leaders. It is certainly not the only cause. Attrition is often caused by a lack of training, a lack of preparation, a lack of clear ministry expectations, a lack of proper placement, and a lack of communication, etc. But very often pride is the source of much unresolved conflict and division in Christian ministries, revealing itself in people who demand to be *right,* who demand to be *first,* who demand to be *seen,* and who demand to be *happy*—demands which can *all* be traced to the root problem of pride.

I'll never forget the day a Christian leader came to visit our family in the Philippines. He was a field director for a missionary sending organization with the responsibility of caring for and directing twenty-six missionary families. I was a novice in those days, and wanted to learn everything I could. "What's the greatest challenge you face in your position of leadership?" I asked. *"Missionaries!"* he exclaimed without hesitation, "because they just can't get along with one another." And then he added a colorful analogy: "Missionaries are like (cow) manure...they're better when they're all spread out!"

Sadly, ask any Christian leader, and they will give you a similar answer. The spiritual, emotional, and financial pressures of ministry often amplify our differences in personality and temperament, our approaches to ministry, our eccentricities, our unique leadership styles, our cultural expectations, our personal convictions, our character flaws, and our immaturity. And unless we allow ourselves to be formed in humility, these differences will trouble and embitter and cause great harm to the church (Hebrews 12:15). From the root of bitterness grows anger, power plays (often passive aggressive), distrust, suspicion, character assassinations, a critical spirit, indifference (treating others as if they don't exist or don't matter), and all forms of abuse.

Pride is a *serious, serious* threat!

HUMILITY WILL CHANGE THE WAY YOU LIVE

Humility will help make even difficult relationships work because you will become less concerned for yourself and more concerned for others. You will become less defensive and more approachable, less opinionated and more teachable, less distracted and more attentive to the person in front of you, less rigid and more flexible. Listen to James:

> For where jealousy and selfish ambition exist, there will be disorder and every vile practice. But the wisdom from above is first pure, then peaceable, gentle, open to reason, full of mercy and good fruits, impartial and sincere. And a harvest of righteousness is sown in peace by those who make peace (James 3:16-18).

I want this harvest of righteousness, don't you?

Humility will not only change the way you live, but it will also change the way you lead. Humility will form you into a servant leader who takes an interest in the needs and accomplishments of others.

Before we left the Philippines in 2009, I wrote the following letter to pastors and ministry colleagues we had had the honor to serve. As I wrote, I thought of specific men and women and the example of humble service they had set for me and my family.

Many of you pastors and workers have beautifully exemplified the mind of Christ to our family, and we have learned incredible spiritual lessons through your faith.

When you patiently and lovingly cared for the disabled child who will never be able to thank you, when you cared for a spouse through long periods of illness until God worked a healing miracle, when you returned to serve a congregation that had hurt you, when you allowed God to break your pride and then lift you up to a place of spiritual authority, when you returned good for evil even when you were encouraged to seek justice, when you labored faithfully with little recognition or appreciation, when Christ's compassion compelled you to care for the widows and indigent among you, when you served the Lord cheerfully without the nurturing love and support of a companion, when you allowed past mistakes

> Humility will not only change the way you live, but it will also change the way you lead. Humility will form you into a servant leader who takes an interest in the needs and accomplishments of others.

to humble you and make you the person of prayer and anointing you are today, when you consistently gave the Master your best through crisis and poverty, when you stood for truth and righteousness even when it was most inconvenient and unpopular, when you gave up your sideline in order to devote yourself to the ministry, and when you've served God in quietness and meekness in your humble place, we've noticed! More importantly, Heaven has recorded it all. I can hardly wait for the day Jesus crowns you! I want to be there when you receive your glorious reward for *living out* the mind of Christ. Thank you for your example!

This is what humble leadership looks like! And these are the kinds of men and women others want to follow.

Humility makes men and women *other*-oriented. It will produce leaders who are not consumed with themselves, but leaders curious about what God is doing in and through others.

When humble leaders stand before audiences, they overcome self-consciousness and fear by thinking of those before them: *Who are they? What burdens are they carrying? What have they accomplished for the Lord? What sacrifices have they made? What experience have they gained? What have they learned?* Humble leaders are thankful for the gifts and graces they see in others, but humbled by those they fail to see in themselves.

Humble leaders acknowledge others for their character, their accomplishments, their successes. They do not flatter for personal or ministry advantage but give honor where it is due.

Humble leaders understand that people have a God-given desire to be known—to be heard, to be taught, to be seen, to be led, to be valued. But thinking of and acknowledging others is not just something great leaders do—it is something they *are*. They are other-oriented leaders because they have an other-oriented heart and think in other-oriented ways.

HOW THEN SHALL WE ATTAIN THE HUMBLE MIND OF JESUS?

This is a most important question. We need Christ's mind because we are often challenged by the things that challenged him. Those we are called to serve are not only needy, but often selfish, rude, ungrateful, and at times show very little consideration for our weariness and need for solitude. We are often criticized. Our conversations are often interrupted, and our recreation is cut short by their demands and emergencies.

Like Jesus's disciples, our disciples are also "slow of heart to believe" but quick to fall into the traps of the enemy. Without the mind of Christ, we'll lose his tenderness of heart and cheerfulness of disposition, and our ministries will be more characterized by irritability than humility. So how do we get this mind? Is it even possible? His humility was so deep, so vast; but we are so tempted by self-will, self-sufficiency, selfish ambition, and self-promotion.

To have the humble mind of Jesus, you will have to choose it—"Have this mind" (Philippians 2:5). When you are tempted by self-righteousness, self-gratification, self-promotion, and the other self-sins, choose the way of Jesus. Jesus chose to lay aside His reputation, and God rewarded Him with a name (Philippians 2:9). And we should choose humility because in God's time and for his glory our humble road will also lead to exaltation:

A Simple Humility

> Humble yourselves, therefore, under the mighty hand of God so that at the proper time he may exalt you (1 Peter 5:6).

Second, to have the humility of Jesus you will have to receive it by faith; you simply can't produce it in yourself. Pride is a deep root that cannot be pulled up with a few self-help principles. Only the life of Jesus within you can deal with pride and form his humility in you.

Because Christ now indwells us by his Spirit, there is a sense in which each believer already *has* the mind of Christ, but we must yield to it; we must possess it by faith. Paul reminded proud-minded Corinthians, "But we have the mind of Christ" (1 Corinthians 2:16). They had the mind of Jesus because they were in him and he in them, but now they needed to reckon on it. The deposit of Christlike humility had been made in them, but now they needed to make the withdrawal; now they needed to live it out. The problem with the Corinthians was not that Jesus didn't indwell them, but that in their decision-making they were crowding him out.

> **Without the mind of Christ, we'll lose his tenderness of heart and cheerfulness of disposition, and our ministries will be more characterized by irritability than humility.**

Third, you must cultivate humility by opening your heart to the Word of God and to the voice of the Holy Spirit. I'm convinced that for humility—like any grace—to permeate your nature, you will have to exercise it. Sometimes this will mean keeping quiet, and sometimes speaking up. Sometimes this will mean preferring others ahead of you, and sometimes it will mean accepting honor. Sometimes it will mean working behind the scenes, and sometimes it will mean working in the public eye. The Lord will teach you what it looks like for you.

You will have to commit to God that no matter what it costs, you want him to cleanse every element of pride from your life and ministry, and then take every opportunity as a chance to die! If you're willing to listen, the Holy Spirit will show you your ways of thinking and acting which are hindering his blessing and provide plenty of opportunities for you to die to yourself.

George Mueller, known for his great faith and his ministry to thousands of orphans in nineteenth century England, was asked the secret of his fruitful service to the Lord. "There was a day when I died, utterly died," he answered. As he spoke, he bent lower and lower until he almost touched the floor. "I died to George Mueller—his opinions, his preferences, his tastes, and his will—died to the approval or blame even of my brethren and friends—and since then, I have studied only to show myself approved unto God."

As Becky and I have worked with ministry colleagues overseas and here at "home," there have been numerous occasions when God has dealt with elements of pride in us—elements we weren't aware of until he revealed them to us. Though we surrendered our lives to the Lord many years ago, we've been tempted by many of the "self" sins mentioned in this chapter. And I've been too impatient, too unfair in my expectations, too stingy with honor and praise, too self-conscious, and...my list could go on and on! Each realization has caused us to come to the cross for fresh cleansing and a fresh filling.

You'll never outgrow your need to die, but God's Word promises that those who fall into the ground and die will bear much fruit. It'll happen. Just ask a little-known disciple named Matthias (Acts 1:21-26).

The little that we know of this humble man tells a fascinating story. Though God would eventually choose him as one of the apostles, this quiet guy at the back of the room would first be tested by *being overlooked*.

One day, we don't know when, Matthias heard about a preacher, an Elijah-like character, who preached by the Jordan River. He listened to John's sermons and was likely converted and baptized under his ministry; but when one better than John came along, Matthias became a devoted follower of Jesus.

Though, when Jesus chose his team of apostles, Matthias was not a first round pick (Judas was chosen over him!), yet he and Jesus became *inseparable*. Luke tells us that Matthias was one who "accompanied us during all the time that the Lord Jesus went in and out among us, beginning from the baptism of John until the day when he was taken up from us." Matthias was not a position seeker, but a committed Jesus follower. Like most people, he may have felt overlooked at times, but he just kept following.

Matthias heard every sermon of Jesus. He witnessed the miracles. He was likely one of the seventy that Jesus sent out to preach. He endured the hardships of discipleship. He ate where Jesus ate and slept where Jesus slept. He probably experienced Jesus' loving rebukes. He saw Jesus die and was a witness to his resurrection. Matthias missed nothing.

Matthias is never recognized in the Gospels as an up and coming leader. There is no indication of the spiritual stature he will someday have. But what I love about Matthias is that he just keeps showing up. Day after day he is there, on the good days and bad days, on the exciting days and the disappointing days. You just can't get rid of this guy. Jesus doesn't have to promise him a position to keep him around. He's not waiting for a vacancy!

Even after the ascension you cannot shake this guy! And that's why he's there in the upper room with the apostles as they pray and wait for the "promise of the Father."

Then…in a moment, after 1,000 days of showing up and following Jesus, Matthias gets picked by the Holy Spirit to be an apostle. God, "who knows the hearts," picked him to serve the newly-formed church in a special way. Matthias hadn't asked for it. I'm sure he was humbled and probably frightened by his selection. But he was chosen among the twelve to be a special witness.

One church tradition says that Matthias went to Ethiopia as a missionary and there became a martyr. There is nothing else said of him in Scripture. It seems that even after he was chosen to be an apostle he remained his quiet self. But this man of God is an encouragement and a challenge to all who sometimes get overlooked, for "God resists the proud, but gives grace to the humble."

May the Lord help us to be faithful as Matthias was. May he sanctify our ambitions and give us the heart of a humble servant—a heart content with any office, or no office, so long as we get to be a part of his expanding kingdom!

Perhaps you would want to pray this prayer with me:

> *Father, I have seen that the greatest hindrance in my spiritual journey is pride. I'm done with excuses. I'm finished blaming others. I wholly offer myself as a living sacrifice to you. With the psalmist I pray, "Create in me a clean heart, O God." With Paul I look to the cross and believe that "I have been crucified with Christ; it is no longer I who live, but Christ lives in me; and the life which I*

now live in the flesh I live by faith in the Son of God, who loved me and gave himself for me" (Galatians 2:20). I trust now in the cleansing and empowerment of the Holy Spirit, the one promised by Jesus when he said: "If anyone thirsts, let him come to me and drink. He who believes in me, as the Scripture has said, out of his heart will flow rivers of living water." In Jesus' name, amen.

CHAPTER 7

A SIMPLE WORK ETHIC

Let's talk about
working hard.

> "Genius is 10 percent inspiration and 90 percent perspiration." — Thomas Edison

A CALL TO CHRISTIAN MINISTRY is a call to hard work. It's that simple.

Are you ready for the effort required and the energy demanded to serve Christ and his church well? Ministry will involve spiritual warfare as you "wage war" against "rulers, against the authorities, against the cosmic powers over this present darkness, against the spiritual forces of evil in the heavenly places" (Ephesians 6:12). And ministry will often involve mental, emotional, and physical exhaustion too as you serve as a broken person among broken people in a very broken world. Is this what you signed up for?

Are you ready for some early mornings and late nights? Are you ready for the responsibility of caring for people's souls? Are you ready for the interruptions? Are you ready to respond to crisis needs and unexpected events with love?

Paul wrote to Timothy, "Do your best to present yourself to God as one approved, *a worker* who has no need to be ashamed, rightly handling the word of truth" (2 Timothy 2:15, emphasis mine). The one whom God approves is called a *"worker."* Laziness is unacceptable.

In Jesus' parable on the talents, the master commends "good and faithful" servants who work hard and multiply their talents, but condemns the servant who buried his talent as not only "wicked" but… *"slothful"* (Matthew 25:26). This unfaithful servant put up some lame excuses for why he didn't steward his talent well, but Jesus knew that part of his problem was simply laziness. He didn't want to do the necessary work.

Jesus, on the other hand, found himself nourished and sustained by work—by doing the will of his Father and finishing his *work* (John 4:34), for "the night is coming," he said, "when no one can work" (John 9:4). He went about his work with a sense of urgency, and so must we.

On September 22, 1950, Ed McCully, friend of Jim Elliot, who would one day be martyred with him in Ecuador, wrote a stirring letter to Jim. He was a law student working as a hotel night clerk at the time:

> Since taking this job, things have happened. I've been spending my free time studying the Word. Each night the Lord seemed to get hold of me a little more. Night before last I was reading Nehemiah. I finished the book and read it through again. Here was a man who left everything as far as position was concerned to go do a job nobody else could handle. And because he went, the whole remnant back in Jerusalem got right with the Lord. Obstacles and hindrances fell away and a great work was done. Jim, I couldn't get away from it. The

Lord was dealing with me. On the way home yesterday morning I took a long walk and came to a decision which I know is of the Lord. In all honesty before the Lord, I say that no one or nothing beyond Himself and the Word has any bearing upon what I've decided to do. I have one desire now—to live a life of reckless abandon for the Lord, putting all my energy into it. Maybe He'll send me someplace where the name of Jesus Christ is unknown. Jim, I'm taking the Lord at His word, and I'm trusting Him to prove His Word. It's kind of like putting all your eggs in one basket.... Pray for me, Jim.

Many things about this letter are moving, but I'm especially impacted by Ed's desire to live a life of *reckless abandon,* putting all his energy into it! No tepid, half-hearted, one-foot-in-one-foot-out with this guy. He's putting all his "eggs in one basket!" Is it any wonder the Lord used his life *and death* to impact generations of young people? And I'm praying for more single-minded, fully devoted, ready-to-work Christian leaders like Ed today. This is the kind of zeal God blesses.

A CALL TO CHRISTIAN MINISTRY IS A CALL TO INTENSE WORK

After calling believers to "present your bodies as a living sacrifice," Paul captures the effort demanded of the fully surrendered, sacrificial life when he writes these words:

> Having gifts that differ according to the grace given to

us, let us *use* them: if prophecy, in proportion to our faith; if service, in our serving; the one who teaches, in his teaching; the one who exhorts, in his exhortation; the one who contributes, in *generosity;* the one who leads, with *zeal;* the one who does acts of mercy, with *cheerfulness.*

Let love be *genuine. Abhor* what is evil; *hold fast* to what is good. Love one another with brotherly *affection. Outdo* one another in showing honor.

Do not be slothful in zeal, *be fervent* in spirit, *serve* the Lord. *Rejoice* in hope, *be patient* in tribulation, *be constant* in prayer. *Contribute* to the needs of the saints and seek to *show* hospitality. *Bless* those who persecute you; *bless* and do not curse them. *Rejoice* with those who rejoice, *weep* with those who weep" (Romans 12:1, 6-15, emphasis added).

The Holy Spirit wants you and me to know that Christian service is something we've got to *lean into!* I would paraphrase Paul's admonition this way: "Find what God's made you good at and then *do it!* Do it *according to your level of faith.* Do it *generously.* Do it with zeal. Do it *cheerfully.* Do it *sincerely.* Do it *well.* Do it *competitively*—outdoing one another in honor. Do it *fervently.* Do it *hopefully.* Do it *patiently.* Do it with *kindness.* Do it *without bitterness,* and do it with *compassion,* but *do it.* Because *this* is what a fully surrendered life looks like. Give your sometimes *lazy self* a kick in the pants and *do it!*"

Okay, maybe I overdid that last sentence a little, but I do think Paul's language is pretty intense! God has entrusted you with a spiritual gift—a unique ability to edify and beautify the body, but you mustn't assume that the exercise of this gift will be easy.

DO FOCUSED WORK

Notice also that your best work will be *focused* work—either teaching or generosity, for instance, as the *primary* thing, but not *both*. The Spirit hasn't gifted you at everything, so you'll need to ask yourself, "What's the primary work God has for me to do? What is the role he has for me to fill?" Within that work there will likely be many tasks, but one work.

As a young Christian leader, I asked God to give me a focus. I wanted to do one thing well. I prayed, "God, I don't want to be busy with a lot of disconnected things. I ask that you give me *one* focus—*one* main mission by which I can contribute to your kingdom. It doesn't have to be big. I don't need to be recognized. But I want to know that what I'm doing is important in the kingdom of God."

> God has entrusted you with a spiritual gift—a unique ability to edify and beautify the body, but you mustn't assume that the exercise of this gift will be easy.

The Lord answered this prayer, but not overnight. When I first began praying, I really didn't know with certainty what my giftings were. But over time and with experience, my focus became clearer and clearer. Within a few years, I began to realize that I have a gift for leadership and that I wanted to spend my life offering spiritual leadership and training other leaders to lead (2 Timothy 2:2), beginning with my own family, and with a unique focus on the underserved. And I thank God often for giving Becky and me this clear focus. Not everyone appreciates a focused person because focused people end up saying "no" a lot, but I have found that we are most productive when we stay in our lane.

Jesus was an example of focused work; and at the end of his brief but powerful life he could pray, "I glorified you on earth, having accomplished *the work you gave me to do"* (John 17:4). Don't you want to be able to say that too!?

THE HOLY SPIRIT REFERS TO CHRISTIAN MINISTRY AS "THE WORK"

It's interesting to me that the first missionary endeavor was simply called "the work." After the Antioch congregation had done the work of prayer and fasting, "the Holy Spirit said, 'Set apart for me Barnabas and Saul for *the work* to which I have called them" (Acts 13:2). The main "work" was preaching the gospel to the Gentiles, but this "work" involved a lot of other "work"—prayerful planning, purchasing tickets, travel by sea, walking over land, sleeping in uncomfortable places, preaching, walking some more, getting *stoned,* walking some more...you get the picture. There was a lot of "work" to the "work."

When Paul and Barnabas came back to Antioch, they reported on the work they had been sent out to do and had now completed: "And from there they sailed to Antioch, where they had been commended to the grace of God for the work that they had fulfilled" (Acts 14:26; see also 1 Corinthians 16:9-10).

PAUL ADMONISHES BELIEVERS TO DO QUALITY WORK

Work alone is not important to God, but quality work; work that builds carefully on the foundation of the gospel; work that gets the gospel right. "Now if anyone builds on the foundation with gold, silver, precious stones, wood, hay, straw—each one's work will become known" (1 Corinthians 3:12-13a). Paul warns us of a sobering reality, that on judgment day the *quality* of our work will be revealed, "for the Day will disclose it, because it will be revealed by fire, and the fire will test what sort of work each one has done. If the work that anyone has built on the foundation survives, he will receive a reward. If anyone's work is burned up, he will suffer loss, though he himself will be saved, but only as through fire" (1 Corinthians 3:13-15).

We'd better be sure we do work consistent with the truth revealed in the gospel. To add or take away from God's Word, mix in human opinions, serve with wrong motives, or serve without love, these are works of "wood, hay, or straw" that will not stand the test of judgment day fire.

If I make disciples of myself or my personality, but not wholly of Jesus, that's wood. If you lead worship in a way intended to put the spotlight on you or lead that Bible study without a prepared heart and mind, that's hay. If we're shoddy in our work or exercise the "spiritual gift" of grumbling and complaining, that's straw.

On the other hand, when you "Do your best to present yourself to God as one approved, a worker who has no need to be ashamed, rightly handling the word of truth" (2 Timothy 2:15), and do your work, not under compulsion but "heartily, as *for the Lord* and *not for men*" (Colossians 3:23, emphasis mine), this is gold, silver, and precious stones.

When I do good work for the glory of God even when no one is watching, that's gold. When you humbly do the thing that needs to be done which no one else wants to do, that's silver. When we offer a cup of cold water in Jesus' name, or give generously to orphans, widows, and immigrants when only God knows our sacrifice, that's precious stones.

And when we stand before the Lord Jesus, and his holiness kindles the fire under the pile of works we lay before him, whatever isn't pure will be consumed, and whatever is left will be celebrated and rewarded. For the vast majority of Christians, myself included, the pile of works we started with will be considerably smaller when the burning is over, but *how* much smaller depends on the *quality* of our work.

Let us, then, "be steadfast, immovable, always abounding in the work of *the Lord,* knowing that *in the Lord* your labor is not in vain" (1 Corinthians 15:58, emphasis mine).

The New Testament has so much to say about work:

Those who aren't busy enough with work are to be rebuked:

> For we hear that some among you walk in idleness, not busy at work, but busybodies. Now such persons we command and encourage in the Lord Jesus Christ to do their work quietly and to earn their own living (2 Thessalonians 3:11-12).

But those who are distracted by *too much* work are also rebuked:

> But Martha was distracted with much serving. And she went up to him and said, 'Lord, do you not care that my sister has left me to serve alone? Tell her then to help me. But the Lord answered her, 'Martha, Martha, you are anxious and troubled about many things (Luke 10:40-41).

Jesus' tender rebuke is a cautionary note for those of us who neglect Sabbath and the healthy rhythms of work, worship, rest, and recreation. Jesus rebuked Martha for working to the neglect of her soul. Work had become her identity—a little god in her life replacing affection for Jesus and his Word. This is a temptation many Christian leaders can understand.

It's especially important for ministry families to find a healthy balance between work and play. There are seasons when the demands of ministry will stretch you to your limits, but these seasons must be followed by intentional rest and renewal. Jesus often pushed his disciples to exhaustion, just as he will us; but he also knew when it was time for a break, "And he said to them, 'Come away by yourselves to a desolate place and rest a while.' For many were coming and going, and they had no leisure even to eat" (Mark 6:31).

As missionaries, our family has rarely had the luxury of long vacations, but after a season of hard work we have often taken long weekends away from the demands of ministry. While serving in the Philippines, we'd sometimes spend a day or two at a missionary guest house, or occasionally at one of our favorite resorts, making wonderful memories with our children and sometimes other missionaries. The practice of breaking away has been good for our children, and for Becky and me too.

PRACTICAL LESSONS ON DOING PRODUCTIVE WORK

For the rest of this chapter, I want to talk to you about some of the most important lessons the Lord has taught me about becoming more productive in my work:

First, to do more productive work, one must learn to *plod*. The realization that I needed to learn this came to me many years ago in the Philippines. After back-to-back-to-back seasons of ministry "adventure," I entered a season of *intense boredom*. It wasn't that I didn't have anything to do, but that what I was doing—what needed to be done—wasn't much fun. I didn't have a project in front of me. I wasn't hiking the mountains, visiting churches, training leaders, or dedicating new chapels. Ministry slowed to a crawl. It was tough.

When seasons of life like this come, it's often harder for us to get up in the morning, everyday life becomes monotonous and routine, and ministries which once used to excite us now seem dreadfully laborious. The challenge isn't there like it once was. The zest for life has turned sour. You know what I mean.

During this difficult season I wrote this reflection:

> I had a refreshing talk with a friend (David) about this while in Banaue recently, and he said that many pastors have been feeling the strain of boredom this year. I wonder why? We talked at length about the temptations that go along with boredom—idleness, wandering thoughts, apathy, bad nerves, enormous pressure, etc. It seems ironic but "running" is much preferable to "walking." Maybe that's why we run so much. Maybe that's why we stay so busy even with activities having little to do with our calling. Our running about sometimes acts as a drug to dull the pain of waiting on God, of facing ourselves, and of bearing the heavy spiritual burdens of the kingdom. I'll admit that I'm sometimes afraid of the effort that walking requires—discipline, grit...
>
> In the midst of my boredom, I came across this timely

word from Oswald Chambers in *My Utmost for His Highest:*

> There is no thrill in walking, yet it is the test for all our steady and enduring qualities.... When we are in an unhealthy condition either physically or emotionally, we always look for thrills in life. In our physical life this leads to our efforts to counterfeit the work of the Holy Spirit; in our emotional life it leads to obsessions and to the destruction of our morality; and in our spiritual life, if we insist on mounting up "with wings like eagles" (Isaiah 40:31), it will result in the destruction of our spirituality.
>
> I had not thought so much of the significance of walking in the Spirit...or walking with God.... The Lord is helping me to see in a new and fresh way that the life which truly pleases him is a life of consistency and faithfulness and disciplined resolve even when there is little to inspire me.... Walking is tough. Walking requires patience and perseverance. Walking builds character. Walking makes us better men and women and will accomplish some purpose of God in our spiritual lives.

Missionary, cultural anthropologist, and social reformer to India, William Carey, is often called the "father of modern missions." Over his forty-one years in India, he saw "only" 700 converts, but his ministry is said to have been a turning point in Indian culture. Carey translated the Bible into seven languages, founded primary schools—which expanded to include girls in an era when the education of girls wasn't accepted in India—opened Serampore University, produced textbooks and dictionaries to serve both primary school and college-level students, campaigned to end the practice of Sati (widow burning), and made significant contributions to botany. William Carey lived one of the most productive lives I've ever read about, and yet toward the end of his life he said, "If he (his biographer) gives me credit for being a plodder, he will describe me justly. Anything beyond that will be too much. *I can plod. I can persevere in any definite pursuit. To this I owe everything.*"

"To this I owe *everything*." I read that statement many years ago, and it absolutely changed my way of thinking about work. I began to realize the incredible power of steady, focused work. Lettie Cowman put it like this: "The glory of tomorrow is rooted in the drudgery of today." In other words, if we will learn to do good, steady work even through seasons of drudgery, someday we'll reap the rewards (Psalm 126:6). It's a primary principle of life.

> "I can plod. I can persevere in any definite pursuit. To this I owe everything."
> — William Carey

Becky and I have the joy of seeing this principle play out in our family. After 31 years of teaching, training, correcting, loving, failing, forgiving, and being forgiven, we now get to see our children and grandchildren blossom into the people God created them to be. It's so much fun.

I'm seeing this principle play out right now with the ministry I lead. Eleven years ago, Shepherds Global Classroom started out as a very tiny seed; and today our team serves thousands of underserved Christian leaders in over 37 countries and in 31 languages. How did it happen? *When* did it happen? Little by little, one tedious step at a time, 4,015 days and 96,360 tedious hours of meeting, praying, planning, writing, proofing, creating media platforms, re-writing, one word at a time, translating, through ten seasons. I'm not *sure* when it happened; but we knew the vision was from God, and we just kept at it by his grace. And now we're seeing God do things beyond anything we imagined. The plodding is paying off. It always does, so, "let us not grow weary of doing good, for in due season we will reap, if we do not give up" (Galatians 6:9).

Second, to do more productive work Christian leaders must train themselves to be efficient. During our first few years of ministry, Becky and I would listen as often as possible to Elizabeth Elliot's radio broadcast, *Gateway to Joy*. Of all the missionary stories she told and all the wisdom she presented, nothing helped us more than her oft-repeated counsel, *"Do the next thing."* Hardly a day goes by that this counsel doesn't echo in our ears. What Elizabeth meant was, rather than thinking about our boring or less than desirable situation, we should set our mind and effort on the next good thing that ought to be done.

So if clothes need to be washed, or a book needs to be read, or a letter needs to be written, or finances need to be organized, or a message needs to be prepared, or a friend needs to be prayed for, or a garden needs to be tended, or a sick neighbor needs to be visited, or a spouse or child needs affection, or if we just need to take a nap or sit quietly to think and pray, and if that is the next thing I *should* do, then I should *do that thing*. I shouldn't *think* about doing it...but *do* it and do it without delay.

This is a discipline that will take time to learn, but it will lead to a steadier, more productive, and more joyful life. There are many people today who are about to do something but never get around to doing it. Or by the time they get around to doing it, momentum has shifted, and the opportunity has slipped away. You will do better than that, won't you?

Third, to do more productive work one must sometimes sacrifice the good for the excellent. You live in a world of distraction, with many *good* things competing for your attention and affection; things like Pinterest, hunting and fishing, shopping, talk radio, etc. You will always have to battle the tendency to sacrifice the *excellent* on the altar of the good.

Sports are a good thing in my life. I enjoy playing ball when I can, but I also enjoy rooting for my teams. I enjoy the competitiveness. I enjoy watching world-class athletes compete at the highest levels. But I have learned that *good* things, like sports, can become obsessions which keep me from the *best* things.

Nearly everything which will yield life's greatest joys, our obsessions will steal from us.

Your obsession will steal your mind.

The hours you spend on your obsession are hours you could be spending on pursuits which will add quality to your life—reading for example. Think about this: The average reader can read about 200 words per minute with 60% comprehension. So, if you set a goal to read just 15 minutes a day, you could read 3,000 words per day and over 1,000,000 words per year. If the average book is 30,000 words, you could read 36 books a year!

Your obsession will steal a skill which could promote you.

David's transition from David the shepherd boy to David the king was due, in large part, to his mastery of two skills—the harp and the sling. The harp brought him *before* the king, and with the sling he *became* a king. God has given you skills too, skills he wants to use for his glory; but it's up to you to sharpen them. Imagine the satisfaction you would experience by becoming *better* at what you're *good* at. Think of the opportunities that may come your way.

Your obsession will steal your most precious earthly relationships.

Healthy, fulfilling relationships require tremendous investment. We need to *step up!*

Marriage is hard work, so if you see a strong, affectionate marriage, I can assure you it didn't just happen. Marriages are deepened and strengthened when husbands and wives invest in each other, when they sacrifice short-term pleasures for more enduring ones. Raising children is hard work too (Becky and I have raised five), but show me a father and mother who are close to their kids, and I will show you parents who have learned to moderate their obsessions for their sake.

Your obsession will steal your affection for God.

John Piper constantly reminds us that "God is most glorified in us when we are most satisfied in him," so be careful of obsessing over anything that takes away your affection for Jesus.

Here is an easy test to take if you really want to know where your love is: What do you think about most? What do you spend most of your free time doing? What affects your emotional highs and lows? What fills you with the greatest joy or disappointment? What inflames your passion? What do you spend your money on? What subject dominates your conversations? That's what you love the most.

When I was a sports-loving twenty-year-old, the Lord helped me see that the mastery of marriage, family, and calling would require devotion. And he helped me see that if I didn't keep sports (especially watching sports) in a small corner of my life, it would steal life's most precious things from me. So I began to make changes and set boundaries. I've certainly made mistakes over the years, but by God's grace I'm working hard to keep sports in its place. I can now enjoy my favorite teams with more detachment than I have in the past, and I like the trade-off.

I want you to get the most joy out of life. I don't want you to suffer regret later in life. I seriously doubt that too many people will approach the end of life and say, "I sure wish I'd obsessed a little more over my house or my hobby or my cat or my fantasy football team!" But we may very well wish we had spent more time on the things that matter most. Most of us will wish we had cultivated a closer walk with God and our spouse, played more with our children and grandchildren, and been a better friend. Some might wish they'd volunteered more, gotten an education, or become a better leader or musician or artist or speaker or writer or reader of good books. When we approach the end, we'll wish we had spent time on more excellent, productive, and joy-inducing pursuits.

Here are a few practical tips for pursuing excellent things:

- Don't be a legalist, but let the Holy Spirit teach you through his Word.

- Talk to your spouse and/or to other spiritual guys and gals about this and challenge one another.

- Be willing to moderate anything if you become convinced moderation will ultimately lead to greater joy and productivity.

- Set clear boundaries and hold to them.

To do more productive work, you must learn the grace of detachment. It seems to me that one of the great struggles of many Christian leaders is that we often hold too tightly to our personal comforts. I often hear statements like, "I need my sleep," or "I need my downtime," or "I need recognition," or "I need my comfort food," and so forth. The demands of ministry are great; and discomfort, inconvenience, and interruption are part of what we signed up for. People don't have emergencies on our schedule, they aren't hungry or needy on our schedule, they usually aren't born on our schedule, and they don't die on our schedule, so we need to train ourselves to let go.

Jesus was always thoughtful of his disciples, but as they went about serving the needs of people, he often pushed them to the breaking point to train them in this area of detachment.

It's okay for you to have likes and preferences, but most of these are not as needful as you

> **People don't have emergencies on our schedule, they aren't hungry or needy on our schedule, they usually aren't born on our schedule, and they don't die on our schedule, so we need to train ourselves to let go.**

think. You *need* all of Christ, and how blessed to be satisfied with him! In the context of hardships, like hunger, thirst, cold, etc., Paul wrote these incredible words: "For the sake of Christ, then, I am content with weaknesses, insults, hardships, persecutions, and calamities. For when I am weak, then I am strong" (2 Corinthians 12:10). Though Paul didn't prefer hardship—he wasn't stupid—God said to him, "My grace is sufficient for you, for my power is made perfect in weakness" (2 Corinthians 12:9). You'll discover that grace too!

This brings me to one final and most encouraging thought…

Our best and most productive work comes by working *with Jesus* in the *power of the Spirit*. It's not all up to us! Isn't that great news?

Earlier in his second letter to the Corinthians, Paul, whose authority and motives were under severe attack, commended himself to the church. But notice carefully in the following verses that while the tendency of "Christian" leaders is to commend themselves by their gifts, their charismatic personality, or their accomplishments, Paul commended himself as a "servant of God" in whom the *fruit of the Spirit* and *power of God* are being manifest through the things he's *suffering* for Jesus' sake.

> But as servants of God we commend ourselves in every way: by great endurance, in afflictions, hardships, calamities, beatings, imprisonments, riots, labors, sleepless nights, hunger; by purity, knowledge, patience, kindness, the Holy Spirit, genuine love; by truthful speech, and the power of God; with the weapons of righteousness for the right hand and for the left (2 Corinthians 6:4-7).

The highest commendation of one's life and work is this: *that it is marked by the Holy Spirit!* Looking carefully at these verses, I think Paul is clearly saying that every positive quality in his life and ministry can only be explained by the Holy Spirit. I'm afraid that hasn't always been true in me; but I want it to be, don't you? This is the kind of work that will have eternal impact, and after our life's work is completed we'll be able to say with Paul:

> I have fought the good fight, I have finished the race, I

have kept the faith. Henceforth there is laid up for me the crown of righteousness, which the Lord, the righteous judge, will award to me on that day, and not only to me but also to all who have loved his appearing (2 Timothy 4:7-8).

CHAPTER 8

A SIMPLE VISION

Let's talk about knowing
where you're going.

"Thou wilt gather up our little lives and the trickling streams of our influence into the great river of Thy plans and purposes, and they shall go on blessing the universe forever." — Samuel Brengle

VISION WILL MAKE YOU and your spiritual community more focused, efficient, and productive. It's that simple.

It's difficult to capture the concept of vision in one sentence, but here's how I've come to understand it: *Vision is the grace-enabled ability to perceive, plan, and work toward a prayer-saturated, Spirit-directed goal with imagination, wisdom, and perseverance.*

Through the Scriptures, experience, and the example of others, I've learned that there are at least five critical elements or stages of vision. These are: perceiving a need, saturating that need with prayer, forming a plan to meet that need, and then producing results with patience. I want to flesh this out a little bit more in a moment, but first I want to remind us that vision is grounded in the doctrine of human agency.

YOU HAVE AGENCY

While God is a sovereign God whose "counsel shall stand" and who will "accomplish all my purpose" (Isaiah 46:9-10), yet "he has created the world in such a way that human beings have agency within it!" [1] It's a *fundamental* Christian doctrine you must embrace.

God made mankind *to rule* creation *as God's representatives* in the world—his images (Genesis 1:27-28). He made us to govern in a way that reflects his nature, to rule justly as *he* would have done it without us. We were made to cultivate, to conserve, and to employ earth's abundant resources for human flourishing. We were made to think, to explore, to test, to build, and to create new systems, programs, and technologies for the good of humanity. King David rejoiced in our royal status:

> Yet you have made him a little lower than the heavenly beings and *crowned him with glory and honor.* You have *given him dominion* over the works of your hands; you have *put all things under his feet,* all sheep and oxen, and also the beasts of the field, the birds of the heavens, and the fish of the sea, whatever passes along the paths of the seas. O LORD, our Lord, how majestic is your name in all the earth! (Psalm 8:5-9, emphasis mine).

And what is true in natural things is also true in spiritual things. We are not helpless. We can choose to do something about the brokenness we see around us. We can serve the underserved. Jesus commanded us to "make disciples," which tells me that disciples don't just happen, they are *made!* We can make them.

We have agency.

We can pray, and our prayers of faith will have a mighty impact (James 5:16). We can lead, and our wise leadership will revitalize struggling ministries. We can do well, and our deeds will produce fruit (Galatians 6:9). We can love, and our love can melt hard hearts and change the course of history. We can catechize and train and write letters, and our efforts will shape a generation. Astonishingly, God has chosen to accomplish his purposes *in partnership* with ordinary people like you and me. *We humans have agency!*

Noah walked with God and became God's human agent to preserve life, including a zoo full of animals. Though God was "determined to make an end of all flesh" (Genesis 6:13), he *didn't,* because "Noah found grace in the eyes of the Lord" (Genesis 6:8), and "in reverent fear constructed an ark for the saving of his household" (Hebrews 11:7).

> God made mankind to rule creation as God's representatives in the world. He made us to govern in a way that reflects his nature, to rule justly as he would have done it without us.

Abraham believed God and became God's agent to form a new nation *through whom* all the families of the earth would be blessed (Genesis 12:3).

Moses became God's agent to turn away his wrath and save this new nation from complete annihilation (Exodus 32:33). The Bible tells us that God "relented from the disaster that he had spoken of bringing on his people" (Exodus 32:14) because Moses "stood in the breach before him" (Psalm 106:23).

Phinehas also zealously intervened and became God's agent to stop a plague of divine judgment upon the nation of Israel (Psalm 106:30).

Nehemiah became God's agent to rebuild Jerusalem's broken-down walls in just 52 days (Nehemiah 6:15).

Jesus became God's perfect agent reconciling the world to himself, and entrusted to his church the ministry of reconciliation too—"God making his appeal *through us*" (2 Corinthians 5:18-20, emphasis added).

And the New Testament church is a Spirit-clothed community (Luke 24:49), co-laboring with Jesus to make disciples of all nations. The Scriptures teach: "And they went out and preached everywhere, while *the Lord worked with them*" (Mark 16:20, emphasis mine), and while they *"work[ed] together with him"* (2 Corinthians 6:1, emphasis mine). What an astonishing privilege is ours! As we use every means possible to proclaim the gospel and to serve the hungry, the thirsty, the naked, the sick, and the outcast in his name, we can reckon on him working with us. We *can't* do it without him, but he *won't* do it without us. Through the prayerful, Spirit-filled actions of the church, God is making all things new.

As I said, we see agency even in the Great Commission itself. Jesus commanded us, "Go therefore and make disciples of all nations" (Matthew 28:19). *Make* disciples!? Does it seem a little arrogant to think that we could actually *make a* disciple? I imagine a conversation with Jesus that might go something like this:

Us: "Jesus, we can't make a disciple! I mean, only *you* can do *that!*"

Jesus: "No, you're wrong. I've commissioned *you* to do it! *You* can develop strategies and resources which fit your unique situations. *You* can organize efforts. *You* can create programs, catechisms, and training resources. *You* can mentor. *You* can develop relationships. *You* can love people intentionally. I've authorized *you* to do it."

Us: "But Jesus, I thought all we had to do was pray."

Jesus: "Well, prayer is vital, but there's certainly more to it than that. Use your collective gifts, imaginations, and creativity. For crying out loud, be creative! Don't limit your methods to things which have already been done, and don't throw methods out *just because* they've already been done. If it's still working, keep doing it. But I can do new things, too, to meet the new situations, new challenges, and the new demands of a new generation."

Us: "But Jesus, you told us just to baptize and teach."

Jesus: "Oh, but there's 1,000 ways to teach!"

Of course this is a made-up conversation, but I believe it's exactly what Jesus meant. When I see how the apostles worked out the Great Commission, I'm convinced that's what he meant. Even in the first generation, the New Testament church, led by the Spirit, was quite creative:

They started house churches…a new thing!

They started feeding programs to serve neglected widows.

For a while, they created a common fund, and then stopped it after it began to be abused or was no longer necessary.

They organized church leadership into elders and deacons.

They formed the love feast.

They founded a missionary enterprise.

Paul started a non-formal gospel training school in the hall of Tyrannus in Ephesus.

He also initiated a relief effort for a famine in Jerusalem.

God has given his church agency!

I'm confident many Christians have no idea the authority God has vested in them—in *us together as the body of Christ*. They live beneath their privilege. They see needs and hope God will *do* something, not fully grasping that *we* are likely the "something" God wants to do. *We* are his chosen method—his physically present, Spirit-animated body working redemptively in our world.

GOD HAS PLACED YOU IN A UNIQUE CONTEXT

The aim of all we do is to make disciples, but God has placed each of us in a unique *context,* surrounded by unique *needs,* with a unique *ability,* at a unique *moment* in history. And he wants to give his people a unique *focus—a unique way* to glorify him—in the very place he has set us. Each unique situation calls for a unique, creative, and *intentional* response of the body.

While visiting a Muslim tribe in the east African country of Malawi, Gideon Jacobs was deeply moved, not only by their spiritual darkness but by their extreme poverty as well. He learned that two months of the year were called "suicide months," because people would often take their own lives to escape the pain of starvation.

After Gideon traveled back to his home country of South Africa, the burden and compassion he felt for these souls only intensified, and the Holy Spirit began to form a vision in his heart. With the blessing and support of his family and spiritual community, this farmer-turned-missionary has spent the past seven or eight years lifting this tribe out of spiritual and financial poverty. He's trained them in good farming techniques and management, which has led to an abundance of food (suicide months are now a thing of the past!). His daughter has opened a literacy program for adults and an elementary school for children. And Gideon testifies that about 200 former Muslims have found new life in the Lord Jesus Christ. "The Christian chapel is full," he says, "and the mosque is nearly empty!"

Our friends Brennan and Ivon Muir found their unique focus in a desperately needy village in southern Mexico. As they served the Lord in San Gabriel over a six-year period, he began to burden their hearts for the youth of the town. Many were aimless, and even among the Christian youth, there was little understanding of discipleship. Over time, Brennan and Ivon began to envision a discipleship/training program for these young people, and in 2018 they launched a new ministry called Seminario Biblico Esdras, a grass-roots training school making an incredible difference in the lives of dozens of young Latin American men and women.

After returning from the mission field, Steve and Jenny Gardner prayed that God would give them something redemptive to do in their hometown of Frankfort, Indiana. Their hearts were drawn to the desperate, seemingly hopeless condition of girls and women bound by addiction in their community. And after much prayer and planning, they envisioned and then founded a ministry called WeCare Recovery Home. My heart was overjoyed recently to hear testimonies of salvation and deliverance from three of these girls. Steve and Jenny are agents of change.

As Eli and Bethany Fader witnessed the plight of 220,000 South Sudanese refugees living in camps in northern Uganda, most of whom suffer unspeakable psychological trauma from the horrors of war, they envisioned and launched a training ministry especially for pastors. This training ministry is raising up spiritual leaders among the South Sudanese and Ugandans, and these men and women are bringing the hope and healing of the gospel to their traumatized community.

Pastor Ray McCrary Jr prayed that his congregation would begin to have a greater impact in their community. As he studied the demographics around their church, he learned there were over 30,000

Burmese refugees within a five-mile radius, and a vision to serve them was planted in his heart. It hasn't been easy, but God has given Pastor Ray and his congregation a powerful multiethnic ministry among the Burmese. They provide English classes for the adults, tutoring for the teens, and transportation services for those who need help getting back and forth to work. And a strong Burmese congregation has been founded as well.

There are many more examples I could share. My brother-in-law Jeff Keaton founded Renewa-Nation, a powerful, growing ministry God is using to awaken pastors, parents, and teachers everywhere to the importance of providing children and young people with a biblical worldview education. A lady named Anita Brechbill launched a prayer ministry that is impacting countless souls. My pastor, Mark Cravens, began a wonderful podcast several years ago called *"Hope Along the Journey"* that encourages believers with stories of hope. And all of these began with a vision by people who believe in the agency held by Christ followers. They believe Spirit-filled Christians can make a difference.

> It might seem unbelievable to you, but God has given his people creative power—to bring companies, ministries, and services into being that do not currently exist, all by his grace and for the fame of his name.

JESUS IS PRESENT IN THE WORLD THROUGH HIS CHURCH

Each of these stories underscores the truth that God blesses the initiatives of his people. I believe he wants us to think like this. I believe he wants us to live like this. He wants us to get together as his people and to agree together on a redemptive response to the needs around us. He wants the church to unite in prayer, to envision new ministries, and to launch new gospel enterprises. It may look like an in-home Bible study, an English as a Second Language (ESL) program for immigrants, an after-school program for children or teens, a recovery program for addicts, a grocery delivery ministry for the elderly, a community feeding program, a sports camp, a band camp, a "you name it" camp, a business with a mission, or whatever your unique situation calls for. But he wants us...invites us to act.

It might seem unbelievable to you, but God has given his people creative power—to bring companies, ministries, and services into being that do not currently exist, all by his grace and for the fame of his name. There are endless things yet to create, and he is raising you up to play a part. Not by yourself, but with his Spirit and the body of Christ he has placed around you. Jesus said:

> Truly, truly, I say to you, whoever believes in me will also do the works that I do; and greater works than these will he do, because I am going to the Father. Whatever you ask in my name, this I will do, that the Father may be glorified in the Son (John 14:12-13).

In that same conversation with his disciples, he said:

> You did not choose me, but I chose you and appointed you that you should go and bear fruit and that your fruit should abide, so that *whatever you ask the Father in my name, he may give it to you* (John 15:16, emphasis mine).

In the context of John 15, this seems to mean that whatever we ask for as we abide in Christ, as we abide in his Word, as we abide in his love, as we keep his commandments, and as we ask in his name...*he will do it*. He will honor our agency. I've learned this firsthand.

In April 2012, I was traveling with other missionary trainers through East Africa, teaching a diverse group of pastors and laypeople in small villages and in very rustic settings. In each place, pastors and Christian leaders gathered under the shade of mango trees, under simple makeshift shelters, under tents. It was a wonderful, eye-opening season of ministry. These men and women who had had almost no access to theological training were eager students. I was often amazed by their spiritual depth and insight, but also saddened over their lack of resources. And as we taught, it became evident that some of the pastors and leaders we were training had the heart, the capacity, and the gifts to teach as well. They didn't really need us. They needed us to equip them to do what we were doing.

One beautiful morning in a village in Mozambique, I sat on the porch of a rustic mission house with an opened Bible before me. A salty breeze from the Indian Ocean rustled gently through the coconut palms, while a farmer cultivated his pineapple garden close by. The passage I was reading was John 13, and as I read, I was struck by a phrase from the story of Jesus washing his disciples' feet. "Do you know what I have done to you...*I have given you an example,* that you also should do just as I have done to you" (John 13:13-15, ESV, emphasis mine).

As I pondered this word, the events of the past days, the men and women I'd been privileged to teach, and this strong desire God had given me to equip Christian leaders, the thought came to me that we could do what Jesus did for his disciples by providing a training resource suited for them and for their context. *What if we had a training curriculum that was theologically robust, but simple, clear, and concise to put into the hands of these hungry pastors? I thought. Wouldn't that be a wonderful way to serve Jesus' body? Wouldn't that be a way we could help to cleanse away the filth (false doctrines) of the church?*

That morning, I sensed the Holy Spirit was saying in my heart that if we would find a way to develop this resource for the sake of his body—as a *service* to his diverse body—he would prosper our efforts.

Over the next few months, God affirmed this calling by providentially bringing together a team of qualified, dedicated cross-cultural trainers and educators to begin the work, and by providing a generous financial gift which carried us for a couple of years as we developed the curriculum. Within a year or so this vision became known as Shepherds Global Classroom.

Since the planting of the first tiny seeds in 2012, hundreds of thousands of dollars have been invested into twenty foundational English courses and numerous translations, equipping leaders to train thousands of men and women in thirty-seven countries. Our free Shepherds Global Classroom app has been downloaded in ninety-one countries. We could have never dreamed eleven years ago how the Lord would bless our obedience. To God be the glory! *He blesses the initiatives his people take in his name.*

FIVE STEPS OF VISION CRAFTING

For the remainder of this chapter, I want to share some personal, practical perspectives on these five critical steps of vision "crafting": perceiving, praying, planning, producing, and persevering. These perspectives flow out of principles from God's Word, what I've learned from other leaders, and what I've experienced myself as I've pursued the vision the Lord has placed in my heart.

The first step for crafting a particular vision is that you and your spiritual community must perceive the need.

Successful gospel enterprises meet needs. Many "visions" never gain traction because they're trying to solve problems that don't exist, meet needs people don't feel, or answer questions people aren't asking. Or perhaps there are other people and ministries already meeting that need just as well or better than we can. We need to be humble here, by acknowledging, appreciating, and building on the work of others. So much time and money is wasted in the kingdom of God by trying to reinvent what has already been invented.

Listen: Listen prayerfully and with an open mind and heart. Listen to what God is saying to you through the words, problems, confessions, needs of others. Listen with your heart.

Learn: Be curious. Ask questions. Gather facts. Perhaps you'll want to do a feasibility study.

Too often we make decisions before knowing the facts. Missionaries have made this mistake often, and pushed agendas without respecting the wisdom and discernment of national leaders. Too often we have given people what *we think* they need, and miss the things they really *do* need.

Love: Whatever we do must be motivated by love.

A second step for crafting vision is to pray privately and collectively for wisdom and discernment.

Too often we rush into projects and programs without waiting on the Lord. Successful visions succeed with the *right people,* doing the *right things,* at the *right time,* so prayer is vital. We cannot assume we know how to do this on our own. But Jesus promised to give "whatever you ask the Father in my name" (John 15:16). And James said, "You do not have, because you do not ask" (James 4:2).

Pray God's Word over the problem or need.

Pray with fasting: I've found that humbling myself through fasting is very effective when seeking wisdom and a path forward.

Pray for clarity of vision: "For God is not a God of confusion but of peace. As in all the churches of the saints…" (1 Corinthians 14:33). The night before Jesus selected the apostles, "he went out to the mountain to pray, and all night he continued in prayer to God" (Luke 6:12-13). And while the congregation at Antioch "were worshiping the Lord and fasting, the Holy Spirit said, 'Set apart for me Barnabas and Saul for the work to which I have called them'" (Acts 13:2). For the early church prayer was vital for clarifying direction, and it's vital for us too.

Pray for practical wisdom: Pray for the skill to know how to accomplish this thing. James reminds us, "If any of you lacks wisdom, let him ask God, who gives generously to all without reproach, and it will be given him" (James 1:5).

Pray with discernment: John admonishes us to "not believe every spirit, but test the spirits, to see whether they are from God" (1 John 4:1). Is this thing of the Lord or just a passing thought?

Pray together: The Holy Spirit was poured out on the early church as "All these with one accord were devoting themselves to prayer" (Acts 1:14). Vision is often birthed in the heart of one person, but it doesn't end there. True vision will resonate in the hearts of others. "Again I say to you," Jesus said, "if two of you agree on earth about anything they ask, it will be done for them by my Father in heaven" (Matthew 18:19).

As you seek wisdom and clarity through prayer, know that this season can sometimes last a while. If, while praying, the burden for a particular project or ministry persists, keep moving in that direction. But remember that God's timing is just as important as his will.

A third step for crafting your vision is to plan well.

A vision without a plan is just a dream, and the world is full of dreamers. Planning is hard work, and the larger the vision the more important the planning. But if God has put a burden on your heart, he will help you work out initial steps. God blesses faith-filled planning.

Explore: Depending on the project, you may need to take an exploratory trip to "spy out the land"—to assess the need and find a wise path forward.

Ask critical, practical questions: What? When? Where? Who? Why? How? Assume nothing and be as thorough as you can be.

Work out clear processes: Do so if you can. Be as specific as possible.

Develop a budget: God-sized visions are always bigger than our resources, but counting the cost is important to faith and fundraising.

Assign tasks: Delegate responsibilities and clarify each person's assigned role.

Set specific goals: Set specific dates for goals to be reached.

The more important the mission, the more important the planning and preparation.

The fourth step in crafting your vision is the production stage.

Once your team has perceived, prayed, and planned, it's time to act. Now that you've aimed, it's time to pull the trigger.

Act boldly: William Carey said, "Expect great things from God. Attempt great things for God." Once you believe you have received clarity for a particular ministry or project, it's time to step out.

Act as quickly and decisively as your situation calls for: Tentative action in a leader will demoralize and dishearten God's people, so don't delay what doesn't need to be delayed. Through procrastination, momentum is lost, morale suffers, and people lose their nerve. But grace will flow to us when we begin to act.

Act in unity: Be "eager to maintain the unity of the Spirit in the bond of peace" (Ephesians 4:3).

Act sacrificially: True vision will cost you, the visionary. There's no such thing as a vision that *everybody else* pays for! God will bless you with the provisions you need once you've put your own life, your gifts, your time, and your resources on the line. Never complain about your sacrifices. At any cost, they are a small price to pay for meaningful work.

Act in faith: Take the first steps, even when you don't know how the Lord will provide for the next. The sea of impossibilities will begin to part as God's people begin to step in faith (Hebrews 11:29). I've seen it time and time again.

Act with humility: Know that corrections and adjustments will have to be made along the way.

The fifth step in crafting vision is the persevering step.

Every noble work in the kingdom of God requires persistence and perseverance.

Expect criticism and opposition: Not everyone will understand or appreciate what you're doing. Some may even hate what you're doing, so it's important to stay close to Jesus and keep your eyes on the prize. Don't flinch!

Expect problems and temptations: Stand firm. Don't quit!

Evaluate and adjust: Adjust to new information and challenges.

Encourage your team: Effective leaders understand the power of authentic optimism—optimism rising from you out of confidence in God's calling.

Endure to the end: Follow through is vital, and the real test of a visionary is that he/she doesn't quit when things get hard. They know how to plod.

NEHEMIAH WAS AN AMAZING VISIONARY

Each of these briefly-stated principles for crafting vision can be clearly seen in the life of Nehemiah.

Nehemiah *perceived* the "trouble" and "shame" of Israel's remnant and the "broken down walls" of Jerusalem after one of his brothers and certain other men came from Jerusalem to visit him in Susa. At this heartbreaking report he "sat down and wept and mourned for days, and...continued fasting and *praying* before the God of heaven" (Nehemiah 1:3-4).

Through prayer Nehemiah reminded God of his Word and his promises, and through prayer his faith was strengthened, and a bold vision began to form in his heart. Through prayer he became convinced God was calling him to do something about the problems in Jerusalem.

At last, he prayed for success and for mercy in the eyes of the king. And God answered his prayer.

Nehemiah's prayers then turned to *planning*. He planned his trip. He'd need a certain amount of time. He'd need endorsement letters to present to the governors of the province beyond the river. He'd need supplies, so he asked for a letter ordering Asaph, the keeper of the king's forest, to provide timber. He'd need housing, officers of the army, and horsemen. And he was able to secure these things too.

Nehemiah was a masterful planner and organizer. When he got to Jerusalem, he jumped on a horse and began to inspect the damage. He took secret night trips around endless heaps of rubble, some of them impassable. While he rode and measured and thought, he worked out a rebuilding plan. He thought of a way to organize and compartmentalize the work, to divide it into sections, to assign each section to a family or group, and therefore to simplify the vision for others to understand and believe in. When he communicated his plan with the leaders of the remnant, they bought in.

This is the genius of vision. Good leaders can break complicated things down into simple, clear, orderly, "bite-sized" parts or processes so people are able to envision how things could be done. They're able to envision not only the big picture, but also the part *they* will play. And suddenly the impossible seems possible. Everybody knew this rebuilding project wouldn't be easy. They knew they'd need grace, divine provision, divine protection, and divine strength, but for the first time they imagined how this seemingly impossible project could be done. Before Nehemiah came along, all they saw was a mountain of rocks; but now they saw it as something that could be restored.

Nehemiah not only perceived, prayed, and planned, but he and the people *produced* and *persevered*. The people went to work with heart and high morale, but it didn't take long for challenges to arise. Had Nehemiah not responded to these challenges with wisdom, the work would have stopped. The vision would have died. He set up guards to protect the people from threats, stationed people by clans with weapons, resolved injustices, sacrificed his own provisions to help others, and refused to be distracted by opposition. Most importantly, he and the people continued to experience the favor of God, pushed through the hard times, and completed the walls in just fifty-two days! A monumental accomplishment! And a model accomplishment for each of us.

Years ago, while reading his biography, the quote by Samuel Brengle placed at the beginning of this chapter captured my imagination. I've never forgotten it. Samuel Brengle was a beloved evangelist with the Salvation Army in the days of D. L. Moody, and there were moments he was tempted to be discouraged by the small turnout for his evangelistic meetings, while Moody was preaching to thousands, sometimes in the same city at the same time! But then he recalled that his life mattered, not because of the size of his ministry, but because he was convinced that God will "gather up our little lives and the trickling streams of our influence into the great river of (his) plans and purposes, and they shall go on blessing the universe forever."

I don't know what God is putting in your heart to do, but I know he's chosen you and is preparing you for something—something unique, something strategic, something fitted just for you. He's given you agency—you, together with the body of Christ he's placed around you. And even now he is merging your little life, your trickling stream, your little vision with his immense, eternal plan. It's unbelievable, but it's true!

CHAPTER 9

A SIMPLE LOVE

Let's talk about how
you're going to treat people.

> "His look of love went everywhere,
> And lives were changed when he was there,
> Hungry eyes and hungry souls felt his embrace.
> He stooped to mend each crippled child,
> His healing touch was strong but mild,
> And like this man of Galilee I want to be."
> — Gloria Gaither

YOUR SUCCESS AS A CHRISTIAN LEADER will greatly depend upon your love for people. It's that simple.

Several years ago, a dear Filipino pastor friend bought a new (to him) car. One afternoon, he started the car with the intention of backing out of his small carport. He was new to driving this stick shift, and something went wrong. The car lurched forward, knocking over a heavy, steel-framed whiteboard which crashed down upon his two-year-old grandson. Horrified, he rushed to the boy and took him in his arms, but it was too late. The child died from the severe blow to the head.

In the days that followed, there were immature believers and even some family members who cast blame upon this pastor. Some were embarrassed by his carelessness and kept their distance. The cruelty of the side glances and muted whispers when he was around only added to the crushing grief he felt over this tragic accident.

I visited the Philippines a short time later and approached Pastor Froilan, enveloping him in a long bear hug. "How are you doing?" I asked him quietly. After a long pause, he replied through his tears, "I'm very lonely." My heart was broken with him.

Within the body of Christ, there are many lonely, love-deprived men and women. They've made mistakes, caused irreversible messes, failed repeatedly, and disappointed themselves and others. They wonder how God could love them when it seems no one else does. Perhaps this is where you find yourself right now. May I challenge you to think deeply of the love of God revealed in Jesus?

Sometimes we wonder how God could love us. But He does! And the greater our assurance of his love, the greater our potential for service to him. Indeed, the level of risk you'll be willing to take, and the quality of service and sacrifice you'll be willing to render for the sake of the gospel, is directly connected to what you think about God and what you believe God thinks about you. You will never risk your life for a God you do not trust. And to the *degree* that you trust his love, to *that* degree you'll be able to love others.

There's a beautiful story in the Gospel of John which demonstrates the way in which God revealed his love to his own and points the way for us to do the same for one another. This story has helped shape my understanding of Christian love.

John begins his account of Jesus' last meal with his disciples like this: "Now before the Feast of the Passover, when Jesus knew that his hour had come to depart out of this world to the Father, having loved his own who were in the world, he loved them to the end" (John 13:1). Then comes the basin and the towel.

The "hour" John referred to was not the hour of Christ's exaltation alone, but his hour of betrayal, of suffering, of loneliness, of rejection, and of death. From a vantage point of history, John looks back to the events of the night of Jesus' final meal with his disciples, then his betrayal and death, and what was still *most remarkable* to John was the love of Jesus—that he demonstrated genuine other-oriented humility and care when his own life was about to be offered. John wants us to know that while Jesus knew full well that *this* hour of sacrifice was upon him, he wasn't consumed with *that,* but with *them*—his own!

The depth of Christ's love is punctuated by his complete lack of self-absorption even when the clouds of suffering were gathering all about him. He wasn't thinking of himself, but *his own*— these who belonged to him, these whom he would leave behind in this world.

GOD'S HEART IS FOR YOU!

The level of risk you'll be willing to take, and the quality of service and sacrifice you'll be willing to render for the sake of the gospel, is directly connected to what you think about God and what you believe God thinks about you.

In this we see the unexpected nature of Christ's love. His heart was for his own when his own heart was being broken. And his heart is for you, too.

His disciples were still in this world. His mind was on them. *You* are still in this world. His mind is on you.

His disciples would remain in the battle—facing temptation, resisting the devil. His mind was on them. *You* are still in the battle. And His mind is on *you.*

He loved his own to the end. And he'll love *you* to the end.

Jesus' demonstrations of love prepared his disciples for the ministry that would follow his death. He loved these men—his own—though they were ordinary, so slow of heart to believe, so weak, so fearful, so fallible, and sometimes incredibly full of themselves. He called them his own though he knew their weaknesses.

Jesus' love for his disciples wasn't based upon their performance. In fact, he knew in a few short hours they would all deny him, forsake him, and cower in fear for their own lives, even while his was being taken from him. His love for his own was completely full and mature before they'd been purified by faith, received the Spirit, worked a miracle, or preached a sermon.

I believe that many Christian young people and leaders alike are led to despair because they believe that God only regards them with compassion and respect when they're good. Satan wants us to believe this...and to drive us to hopelessness. Jesus did not only love these disciples *after* they were mature, or *after* they had experienced Pentecost, but *before*. And this love and acceptance he had for his own preserved them *for* Pentecost.

Jesus loved his own just as they were and not as he knew they would someday be!

Some of you may have grown up in families or churches where love was very conditional—where acceptance, kindness, and respect had to be earned. Jesus' love for his own is a quality that comes from heaven, and it is pure, perfect, and resilient.

There is nothing Jesus doesn't know about you, and yet he loves you and wants to help you. The Lord Jesus loves you just as you are. He knows about your failures, your struggles, perhaps your besetting sin, and yet he loves you still. If you accept his love, he will not leave you in your condition, but his love will transform your life.

Until we have ourselves been stunned and humbled by the redeeming love and grace of God, we will serve him and others with an edge. We will be forceful, manipulative, harsh, demanding, and even angry. Christians who have not been astounded by God's love and grace go out into the world and hurt people!

The most formative passage in my early days as a missionary was a phrase from the Gospel of John. John describes Jesus as "full of grace and truth" (John 1:14). This description of Jesus, in whom truth *and* grace were fully present and perfectly harmonized, *exposed* me, *convicted* me, and *pressed* me to change. I had come to the Philippines with a briefcase full of truth and only a pocket full of grace, a condition I couldn't see until the Holy Spirit began to open my eyes. There were two painful events which took place shortly after we arrived on the field which the Lord used to awaken me. The first involved an inter-denominational worship event.

Town fiesta was a highly-anticipated and exciting annual event for our town. Night after night brought colorful displays of local culture, music, and food. We lived in the small town of Villasis in Central Luzon, on a Bible college campus situated along a busy rural road about 3 km from its center. And even from that distance, we could hear the loud singing and announcements late into the night.

By Mayor Abrenica's decree, one night of town fiesta each year was dedicated to evangelicals and came to be known as "Evangelical Night." Every evangelical church in town was invited to participate. Each church would bring their finest musical talent, and several pastors would be asked to speak to the crowd of perhaps 1,000 or more. What an opportunity to share the gospel in a very public space!

Our first time to attend, Becky and I and our two young children were invited to sit on the platform, and Becky was to sing a special song. We were the new kids on the block—the young missionaries from America—and treated as guests of honor, a privilege, which to my great shame, I did not appreciate. The faculty and students from our Bible college were present in the audience as well.

As the evening wore on, I became increasingly uncomfortable with the music and worship. One of the livelier Pentecostal churches led the worship that evening, and the music was deafening, and to me, wild. The bigger-than-life speakers situated right behind us weren't helping, of course. But when the little dancing girls came out with their tambourines to accompany the band, my traditional, conservative, Methodist self protested. It felt *provocative,* though I'm sure now that it wasn't.

> Until we have ourselves been stunned and humbled by the redeeming love and grace of God, we will serve him and others with an edge.

I completely overreacted. "Righteous indignation" boiled over. *"I need to make a statement!"* I thought. *"I need to let our Bible college students know that I stand for holiness!"* And before wisdom could prevail, I took Becky and our children by the hand and we exited the platform, got into the van, and headed for home.

I'd made a *statement.* I'd *taken...my...stand.* I was even kind of proud of myself...for a few minutes. But something just didn't seem right about what I'd just done. I began to feel ashamed, but tried to suppress the negative thoughts and emotions.

On the short drive back to our campus, Becky was quiet. *This is not good*, I thought. And in the silence, God *smote* my heart with conviction. I knew that what I had just done didn't measure up to the "grace and truth" life of Jesus. As I drove along, shifting, downshifting, dodging the fiesta crowd, I became aware of my own arrogance and pride and of my lack of grace for these brothers and sisters who had welcomed us. *What...who did I think I was anyway?*

I'll never forget the word spoken to my heart by the Holy Spirit: "Son, I didn't call you here to fix people, but to love them and to make disciples as I give you opportunities. But if you won't love people, I can't use you here." I was so ashamed. In the hours that followed, I asked the Lord and Becky to forgive me and begged God for another chance to show those pastors the same kindness and respect they had shown me.

A short time later, I had the opportunity to speak to many of these same Christian leaders at a joint ministerial fellowship. This time I came with a different attitude, and from a place of love and acceptance I could see them for the sincere, devoted men and women many of them were.

As I reflected on this event in the coming days, I became more aware of my tendency to stand for what I believed was true, but without grace. I tended to judge my brothers and sisters in my heart, to impute motives, to put unkind labels on them, and to harbor suspicions of people without getting to know them. It was a partial awakening.

A second painful event happened a short time later, and it led to a turning point in my life. It won't seem like much on paper, but it was a cataclysmic event in my spiritual life.

One of our Filipino pastors, a man whom I highly respected, came to visit our campus for a few days of quiet spiritual retreat. During his visit, and at his invitation, I offered a word of advice I would only later see as most insensitive and unkind—advice which, had he followed, would have brought hardship to his family.

Several weeks later when we met again this brother took me aside and handed me his resignation from our ministry. I was shocked and devastated! "Why!?" I asked. "Why are you resigning!?" He addressed the inconsiderate counsel I had given weeks before and said that after much reflection he and his wife had decided, "We just can't work with a man who does not love."

"What do you *mean?*" I protested.

We talked for hours, and in those moments the Holy Spirit helped me see myself and my heart as I had never seen it before. I loved God and I loved the Scriptures, but in my relationship with my family and others, I lacked grace. I wept at what I saw. And as I humbled myself, I experienced a cleaning of my heart as I had never experienced before. It was a turning point in my relationship with God and others, *a new step* into a more fruitful Christian life. And, by the way, my brother forgave me and didn't resign after all.

These two experiences of divine chastening opened my eyes to the truth of John 1:14, "The Word became flesh...*full of grace and truth.*"

YOU WILL NEED A RESILIENT, ENDURING LOVE

As you navigate this world, you will be called upon to love those around you,

- when you are irritated

- when you are misunderstood

- when you are tired

- when you are maligned, overworked, underpaid, and unappreciated.

As you work with people, one of the greatest temptations you will face is the "root of bitterness" (Hebrews 12:15). Watch out for it. Christian ministry is a battlefield, and you *will* be wounded. What will you do then? First, you will remember that "we wrestle not against flesh and blood, but against principalities and powers." And then you will choose love!

The most challenging choices you will ever make will be to assume the best in others, to overlook faults, to yield to the opinions and decisions of the body, to honor and protect the reputations of those you disagree with, to "welcome" (Romans 14:1) those with different convictions and scruples, and to sometimes confront, rebuke, and discipline. But all this and more is what the Bible means by love.

> A new commandment I give to you, that you love one another: just as I have loved you, you also are to love one another. By *this* all people will know that you are my disciples, *if you have love for one another*" (John 13:34-35, emphasis added).

The world will not recognize you as a disciple of Jesus by your doctrine, but by your irrational forgiveness when you are hurt. Your colleagues will not recognize you as a Christian by your outward appearance, impressive teaching, or beautiful prayers, but by the kindness you demonstrate when you are embarrassed, by the grace you show when their carelessness has cost you, and when they see you treat people with respect for no good reason and when nothing's in it for you.

Many of you who are reading this today have been trained in wonderful institutions by some of the most gifted servants. You have been saturated with excellence and surrounded by majestic music, skilled communicators, and beautiful facilities. You've lived in a kind of stained-glass Christian atmosphere, interacted daily with exceptionally intelligent people, and enjoyed uplifting, tasteful worship.

Beware! These privileges and blessings make this matter of loving people more difficult. You must develop the mind of Christ—the mind of a servant. You must hold loosely to ideals, and love people right where they are. You must wrap your arms around people who are spiritually ignorant. You must be patient with "bad" theology, suffer long with some sensational beliefs and practices, and participate in worship even when songs or worship style aren't your own personal preference on Sunday morning—all without a cynical spirit. You must love people enough to lift them gradually, patiently toward truth, godliness, and excellence! You must be aware of your own weakness and failures.

You'll be called to associate with those who are different from you—the lowly, underprivileged, uneducated—without even a twinge of arrogant superiority or self-conscious pride. You'll have to let go of your pet peeves, your preferences, your tastes, and your securities for the sake of redemption. Some of you will have to take off your suit and tie, while others will need to put them on.

YOU WILL NEED A HOLY BUT MERCIFUL LOVE

John tells the story of an adulterous woman being dragged into the presence of Jesus by a group of religious leaders. She had been caught in "the very act." Her accusers wanted Jesus to assume the role of an earthly judge—a role he had not been given by his Father. There would be a time and place for that in the future, but not now.

Jesus was silent. I think he was silent because, while he knew her sin and didn't in any way excuse it or sweep it under the rug, he couldn't go along with the undignified and dishonest way in which this precious woman was being humiliated. I believe his silence was the silence of a spirit grieved by the attitude of these men.

THERE IS A RIGHT WAY AND A WRONG WAY TO HANDLE SIN

A stand for truth apart from mercy is profoundly incomplete. The scribes and Pharisees appear zealous for holiness, but the spirit of disrespect and disregard for the adulterous woman—treating her as an object of scorn—exposed hearts bankrupt of true Christian love.

Unlike the Pharisees, Jesus treated *every* person, both male and female, as an image-bearer of God and filled with the breath of the Spirit (Genesis 1:26-27; 2:7). He saw each person as part of a royal family, "crowned with glory and honor" (Psalm 8:3-9).

> Jesus never lost sight of the created dignity of every person before him.

Jesus never lost sight of the created dignity of every person before him. He spoke to both men and women with the same kindness and respect. He was attentive to children. He touched the untouchables, befriended unbelievers, answered the prayers of foreigners, fought for justice for the poor and oppressed, sometimes rebuked religious hypocrites for poisoning the well of salvation, paused to listen to the desperate, undignified, embarrassing cries of blind beggars, and forgave even the guiltiest. His love was never naive or undiscerning, but it was generous…merciful.

Religion void of love feels free to treat people in dehumanizing ways when "they deserve it." Imperfect love also treats fellow believers with contempt when they are of a different tradition, and labels them as "dangerous" when we disagree on certain doctrines or lifestyle issues. It treats people with indifference when they're not on "our team." It excludes, marginalizes, rejects. *True Christianity could not be more different.*

Love is always kind, always thoughtful, always considerate, and always compassionate. Love is mindful of the individual and treats them as precious even after they have thrown themselves away.

THE PROPENSITY OF LOVE IS TO DEAL WITH SECRET SINS…SECRETLY

Love will not shine a spotlight when a candle would do, shout through a megaphone when a whisper would do, or use a club when a gentle rebuke would do. And the only people qualified to deal with the sins of others are those who are aware of their *own* sins and weaknesses (Galatians 6:1).

Instead of passing a sentence upon the woman, Jesus passed a sentence upon her accusers. "Let the sinless one cast the first stone!" He didn't excuse her sin. He simply demanded that justice be fairly and righteously applied. In this, Jesus exposed a common sin: a tendency to punish the sins of others while ignoring our own.

There is a place for exposing and rebuking and for dealing directly with the sins of others, but it must always be done with a heart that recognizes itself as a forgiven sinner too. When done right, confronting sin is done more often with tears and a broken heart than with anger and condemnation.

Jesus only broke his silence when they were finally alone. He recognized that what the woman had done was sin.

He called her to repentance.

He gave her hope that her life could go on in freedom from sexual sin. This is love.

And she listened!

And, by the way, Jesus is not only respectful of this woman but also the religious hypocrites. He knew their every hidden sin. He knew every skeleton in their closet. He didn't humiliate the woman, but neither did he humiliate the men. He lets them walk away in silence. That's grace too.

As you enter Christian ministry, you will need a kind of love which values each person, not on the basis of what they have done or the choices they have made or by their status in society, but on the basis of their worth as created, though marred, images of God.

In *Letters and Papers from Prison,* Dietrich Bonhoeffer said:

> Whoever despises another human being will never be able to make anything of him. Nothing of what we despise in another is itself foreign to us. How often do we expect more of the other than what we ourselves are willing to accomplish. Why is it that we have hitherto thought with so little sobriety about the "temptability" and frailty of human beings? We must learn to regard human beings less in terms of what they do and neglect to do and more in terms of what they suffer. The only fruitful relation to human beings—particularly to the weak among them—is love, that is, the will to enter into

and to keep community with them. God did not hold human beings in contempt but became human for their sake. (Bonhoeffer, *Letters and Papers from Prison,* p.12).

Loving this way is divine, but it is not automatic. You must practice! You must train yourself to view every person you encounter as an image bearer of God. You must practice patience. You must practice kindness and respect. You must practice grace and mercy, both for yourself and others.

YOU MUST EXTEND THE SERVANT-HEARTED LOVE OF JESUS!

In the narrative of John 13, the humility of Jesus is mind blowing as he takes a towel and bends down to wash the feet of his disciples—the feet of the very ones who had scolded the woman for washing Jesus' feet with the expensive perfume. They had said in essence, "Jesus, you're not worth all this." And yet, on the eve of his crucifixion, to their shock and humiliation, he took their feet in his own hands and washed them.

What is our response when Christ's love for us is humiliating? Is it like Peter's? *"You will never wash my feet!"* It wasn't Peter's high view of Christ that caused this reaction, but more likely it was a painful rebuke at his own lack of humility. He wouldn't have done what Christ was doing. Or perhaps his refusal came simply from a deep sense of unworthiness; but it is never humility that rejects the grace that God is offering to us, but pride. It's always pride that prevents the grace of God from washing us clean. And just as with Peter, if Christ doesn't wash us clean, we will have "no part of him." No part of him to extend that grace to the people we are called to serve.

Some important things to remember about this servant-hearted love:

Servant love listens.

Too many times we assume the worst in people without hearing their story. Servant love is slow to speak and slow to get angry.

Servant love is patient.

Love is not passive or indifferent in matters of righteousness, but neither is it forceful nor demanding. Jesus showed great respect for his disciples when he looked at them one day and said, "I have many things to say to you, but you're not ready." What a gracious, compassionate love! For Jesus, the person was always more important than getting things off his chest. His students were more important than covering the material. He respected them enough to wait for the right moment to say what needed to be said.

Servant love assumes the best in people until it can't.

Love puts the best construction on their words and actions until it runs out of options.

Servant love is never rude.

It is never cruel and never belittling, even when discipline is called for.

Servant love always offers reconciliation, hope, and a path forward.

Servant love refuses to break fellowship over secondary, nonessential, or tertiary issues.

Love's motto is: "In essentials unity, in non-essentials liberty, and in all things charity."

Servant love grants to others the freedom and space to think.
Love allows them to evaluate, to question, to wrestle with doubt, and even to come up with different conclusions, leaving it to the Lord to correct what needs to be corrected. One day, a wealthy young ruler turned his back on Jesus and walked away. Jesus let him go…no manipulation, no pressure, no caustic remarks. Love allows people to walk away from us without shooting them in the back.

Recently, while in the country of Nepal, I witnessed the servant love of Christ being lived out in the lives of Barnabas and Lydia Pandit. They pastor Harvest Church in the capital city of Kathmandu.

Though they are not wealthy, Barnabas and Lydia are constantly giving to those in need. They are providing food and clothing to an elderly man who has no one to care for him, paying the school fees for the son of a Hindu woman whose husband is a drinker and abuser, building a church largely out of their own money, and so much more.

Barnabas and Lydia are from a Pentecostal background, but their non-sectarian kindness toward Christian leaders from other traditions has won them great respect and goodwill. They bring people together.

God is rewarding the generous love of the Pandits with abundance—abundant influence, abundant friends, abundant blessings. A brother in Ireland has helped the Pandits start a small sewing business through which they earn a small income, but also provide work for extremely poor widows from a Hindu background. Barnabas has also been able to earn good wages by working several days a month as a medical assistant. This work has also provided him many opportunities to connect with underserved pastors all around the Kathmandu valley, and he has brought together a team of pastors from various denominations to launch a training center to serve them.

Barnabas and Lydia emanate the fragrance of Jesus in a culture where the atmosphere is saturated with pungent incense rising from thousands of Hindu shrines. People trust them and follow them because of their love.

YOU WILL NEED A DIVINE LOVE

The kind of love we've discussed in this chapter is not self-generated. It only has one source: "Beloved, let us love one another, for *love is from God,* and whoever loves has been born of God and knows God" (1 John 4:7, emphasis added). To know this love, you must remain in God.

Decide today to receive this love and then to live out this love in your family, in the church, and in the world around you. Allow the compassionate, never-ending, unconditional love of God to astound you, to fill you, and transform you. It will preserve you and make you fruitful in the kingdom of God.

CHAPTER 10

A SIMPLE FRIENDSHIP

Let's talk about my friend David,
and why you need someone
like him in your life.

> "And though a man might prevail against one who is alone, two will withstand him—a threefold cord is not quickly broken." — Ecclesiastes 4:12

I WANT TO TELL YOU more about my friend, David. Sooner or later, you'll need a friend like him. It's that simple.

Anyone who's been around me more than a few days has probably heard me mention the name David Yucaddi, and for good reason. He's about ten years my senior, and has been a tremendous influence in my life.

The Lord has blessed me with several great mentors in various seasons of life and ministry, but the Lord brought David and me together at an extremely formative season of ministry for both of us. My years from age twenty-seven to age forty were spent working directly with him in the Philippines. This was a strategic season in the formation of the ministry David founded (Gospel Light BMC), as well as an extremely formative season of life and ministry for me. I'll forever be indebted for the grace poured into my life through this relationship. I want to share a little of that grace with you, but let's begin with David's story.

David C. Yucaddi was born into the notoriously proud and fierce Ifugao tribe of the Cordillera (mountainous) region of northern Luzon in the Philippines. His hometown of Banaue sits at an elevation of about 3,500 feet, and is nestled in a mountain valley surrounded by rice terraces—terraces referred to as the "eighth man-made wonder of the world." The beauty of the place is impossible to describe and unforgettable.

David's forefathers were headhunters, still killing and being killed as recently as the early half of the last century, as tribes fought one another for dominance. His father, Richardo, provided for his family by wood carving, a craft common among the Ifugaos, and which became more lucrative after tourists began arriving several decades ago. But Richardo walked out on his family while David was still quite young, leaving them vulnerable and in emotional and financial ruin. In the absence of a provider, poverty now became the cruel master of the Yucaddi family, and daily life became a constant struggle for survival.

David carried the pain and bitterness of his father's abandonment into adolescence and young adulthood. As David entered his teenage years he gravitated toward bad company. His natural charisma made him a notorious leader among Banaue's young rebels, and he and his "barcada" (friends) would often walk the streets of Banaue and its surrounding villages searching for mischief. They were known to disrupt wake services and wedding ceremonies by their intoxicated singing, and to sometimes mock and debate missionaries and native evangelists during open-air evangelistic meetings.

David drank a lot, had many "girlfriends," and excelled at gambling through card playing and the popular sport of cockfighting. And his successes only fed his arrogance. Not even marriage to beautiful young Margie and a family of his own could settle this restless life or empower him to change his destructive behavior. I've heard David testify of how he'd promise Margie time after time that he was *finished* with gambling, that he would quit drinking, that he would *end* his adulterous relationships, that he would begin to act responsibly, and that he would become a better provider for their growing family, but he felt *powerless* to change.

Shame often overwhelmed David. Though David had become a successful wood carver by his late twenties, most of his earnings went, not to feed and clothe Margie and their four children, but to support his vices. Their house was nothing more than a shack, their clothes threadbare, their home all but broken, their future…hopeless.

Such was the spiritual condition in which David, now twenty-eight, found himself on a January evening in 1987. After a big gambling win, David and his friends had decided to celebrate their winnings with more drinking and gambling—and this was the *seventh day* of their party. Late in the evening of January 15th, David slipped away from his friends to get some sleep. He desperately needed rest. But as he lay there in the dark, sleep escaped him. Waves of shame washed over him. He thought of Margie and of the pain his unfaithfulness and irresponsibility had caused her, and then of their children, Timothy, Erastus, David Jr., and Cheryl Ruth, and of the suffering his neglect had brought on them. He knew that even at that moment his family was suffering.

David began to sob. He felt hopeless and helpless—helpless to change himself. He had tried so many times to change, but every effort had proven futile. He wondered if there was hope for a man like him.

As he lay there, suddenly his eyes fell on a little Gideon New

Testament lying on a small bedside table. Though this was not a Christian home, somehow one had been placed there. David began to read, and the power of God's Word took hold of his heart. He couldn't put it down. As he read on and on and on, a thought began to grow in his mind that maybe these pages held the answer for him. He followed underlined passages where the gospel was clearly presented, and then his eyes fell on John 14:6, "Jesus said unto him, 'I am the way, the truth, and the life. No one comes to the Father except through Me.'"

"As I read those words of Jesus," David has testified many times, "the thought came to me most forcefully that Jesus could set me free. Somehow, as I read and thought about those words, it dawned on me that Jesus could deliver me. So, in desperation I looked toward heaven and said, God you know how many times I've tried to change myself, and you know that my every attempt has failed. If you really have the power to change me, then I ask you to change me right now. Please change my heart and give me the power to live as I should."

"As I prayed these words," David continues, "I felt a cleansing that I can't explain. I knew in my heart that God had heard me, and I began to weep. I knew something wonderful had happened within me, and I just wept and wept!"

As morning dawned, David decided to put his newfound faith to the test. "I knew that the real test of conversion would be when I left that house in the morning," he says. "You have to understand that I was so addicted to gambling that my hands would literally itch at the sight of a deck of cards, and I knew that my friends were still around the fire gambling. But as I stepped out and saw them gathered there, I knew that God had truly worked a miracle in me, because, for the first time in my life I didn't want to join them anymore. That's when I knew I'd been set free!"

When our family returned from the Philippines in 2009, David presented me with a very special gift. It hangs in my office today, and each time I look at it I am reminded of the power of the gospel that changed not only David's life but the trajectory of an entire family. David entrusted to me a family spear and shield, the shield carved from a single piece of wood inlaid with animal bones and still carrying the scent of smoke from countless wood fires. This spear was used by his ancestors for generations. I treasure these gifts, and especially the undeniable power of the gospel they represent.

The continuation of David's life in Christ is just as wonderful and, in many ways, more dramatic than his conversion. In summary: The Lord brought Margie to faith about a month after her husband, and a few months later opened the door for their family to move to a small Bible college where they would study God's Word and prepare for Christian ministry. The Yucaddi's learned so much about the things of God over the next two years, but most importantly they learned to trust God as their faithful Provider.

In 1989, the Holy Spirit spoke to David from Acts 1:8 and called him and Margie (and now two additional children) back to their Ifugao people with a vision to reach them with the gospel and to plant churches. The ministry they founded together is now called Bible Methodist Gospel Light Church.

Over these decades they've endured incredible hardships, persecution, and intense spiritual warfare but have never wavered from the call of God. In 1999, God fulfilled their vision for a training center where dozens of full-time church planters and pastors have been trained for ministry, resulting (to date) in more than forty established churches among six tribal peoples. Many seemingly hopeless men and women and young people, as David once was, have found forgiveness and deliverance at the foot of the cross, and in the one who said, "I am the way, the truth, and the life."

Among David and Margie's chief joys is the joy of witnessing how the gospel is redeeming their family. Three of their five sons are serving as pioneer pastor, theological educator, and music teacher respectively, and their only daughter, Cheryl Ruth, is an accountant for Gospel Light and helps her father in a multitude of ways!

David and Margie are quick to acknowledge many imperfections and numerous mistakes on their journey of faith. Their lives have not been without struggle. But all that they are or ever will be, they attribute to the redeeming love of God, a love which found them when they had lost all hope.

CALLED TO WORK TOGETHER

Many years ago, and quite unexpectedly, the Lord used the story I've just told to call Becky and me to the Philippines. I was a junior in Bible college and preparing for cross-cultural ministry when God sovereignly placed me in a chapel service where David's conversion story, and the captivating story of a new work of God among David's people, was being told. As I listened, my heart was deeply stirred, and a thought came to me that *it would be such a privilege to work with that man!* It seemed impossible. I had no connections to the speaker or to David, and at some point, as time passed, I assumed I'd just been emotional. But the thought persisted. And as I've looked back on this moment hundreds of times over the years, I've never doubted that this was the moment God chose Becky and me for a special assignment. It would be another four years before the Lord *miraculously* and unmistakably opened the door for this call to become a reality, but it happened!

Young leader, it's important for you to know that God still calls men and women for special assignments. It's also important for you to know that if you wait for him, let him open the doors, let him lead you step by step, he will put you in a place, among people prepared just for you. And when you get there, you'll (eventually) think to yourself, *this fits!* You may not think this right away. You'll need to give yourself time to orient and adjust. You'll always feel insufficient in yourself. And since we live in a broken world, among broken people, there will always be enough trouble to keep you humble. But because God is good, he will send you on a mission shaped just like your personality, your desires, your gifts, and your preparation. And he will use that ministry to shape you more and more into the image of Jesus. This is a beautiful thing we've discovered.

> **You'll always feel insufficient in yourself. And there will always be enough trouble to keep you humble. But because God is good, he will send you on a mission shaped just like your personality, your desires, your gifts, and your preparation.**

WHAT DAVID HAS TAUGHT ME

Working closely with David for twenty-six years has profoundly shaped the way I think and the way I do ministry. I want to share some of this with you in a moment because I want you to know how important it is to learn from others. The Lord has formed us in such a way that we'll never rise to our full potential apart from community—apart from the wisdom, strength, example, experience, and gifts of others.

David and I were colleagues for many years. We've gotten to know and love each other deeply. We've disagreed strongly many times. Sometimes our cultures clashed. We've misunderstood one another, and once, for a season, our relationship was pretty "cool." Neither of us are proud of this; but the Lord helped us through that season, and today our relationship is stronger than ever. I think we both have a deep respect for one another.

David was one of many Filipino pastors and leaders who impacted my life, but there is a uniqueness about his life and ministry that I cannot explain. Here's a short list of the most impactful lessons I've gained from doing life with a first-generation Christian whom God is using to reshape a culture in the mountains of the Philippines.

Give honor where it is due, and God will honor you.

One of the most important lessons I've learned about Christian leadership, I learned from my first encounter with David soon after our family moved to the Philippines in the fall of 1996. A dear Filipino colleague, Rev. Forto, and I traveled six hours through the Cordilleras to David's village—a mountainous, tropical rainforest "paradise" (that's the way I saw it then). I was so excited to finally get to meet him there, but at an elevation of about 4,000 feet, in December, it was much cooler than I expected. It was so cold, even for David, that he gathered some firewood and built a small fire on the cement floor of his little chapel! We huddled around that fire and talked until about 4:00 a.m.

After a couple hours of sleep, I stepped down from the little parsonage and walked twenty feet or so to the edge of the mountain which dropped away hundreds of feet below. The sky was a deep blue, the air was crisp, plants were sparkling with dew in the morning sun, and clouds were floating below and above me. It was breathtaking! But it was a word David spoke sometime in the middle of the night that is burned into my memory.

David had asked why our family had come to the Philippines and what I felt God wanted to do through our ministry. I shared my heart; but at some point, I foolishly referenced some things I had heard about past failures in the work, and how we planned to do better. He listened patiently for some time but then spoke kindly but passionately: "Brother Keep, I'm afraid you have been poisoned! Those who came before you were not perfect, but they were people of truth, integrity, and great sacrifice. They shook the tree and some rotten fruit fell to the ground, rotten fruit you won't have to deal with. *You won't be perfect either, so if you won't honor your predecessor, you too will be a victim.* Those who turned on them will turn on you too. But if you will bless your predecessors in your heart…if you choose to honor them by protecting their reputations and appreciating their contributions and sacrifices, God will surely bless your leadership here. They were the tree shakers, but you will be a builder. You will build upon their foundation."

David's voice was the voice of the Holy Spirit that day, and I took it to heart. From that moment on I have always sought to honor those who've served before me, and I can testify that God does indeed honor those who honor others.

Never compromise the gospel.

Through David's example, I learned that the only solid foundation upon which to build a strong work for God is the simple, clear, unembellished, powerful message of the gospel. "For the preaching of the cross is to them that perish foolishness; but unto us which are saved it is the power of God" (1 Corinthians 1:18). Clever preaching doesn't work. Preaching ourselves doesn't work. The gospel alone has the power to save and sanctify.

David believes traditions and unique denominational distinctives can have a place...*unless* they distort the gospel. I've even heard him express his concern that some Christian leaders might be separating the biblical teaching on "holiness" from the gospel itself, as if they are two separate teachings—as if holiness doesn't flow from faith in all that Jesus has provided for us in the cross. He worries that some of us might be trying to lead people into holiness of heart and life without reference to Christ. He said to me one day, "Some preachers coming from your country talk about *holiness* but not the gospel. They say *holiness* is our distinctive message but seem to separate the doctrine from the gospel itself. I think holiness has become *idolatry* for them." Ouch! I got his point. Even vital doctrines can become idolatrous if the finished work of Christ ceases to be central.

David believes so strongly in the power of the gospel that he's developed a gospel catechism for his people called *The Solid Foundation of Faith for Salvation*, which is reviewed in nearly every conference and Bible camp.

Disciple with the Word of God.

From David, I learned that jargon and clichés and extra-biblical rules are not helpful when it comes to *true discipleship*. One day he observed, "You know, Brother Tim, I've noticed something very important regarding discipleship. I've noticed that when pagans are introduced to the gospel, and then respond in repentance and faith, the bondage of sin is broken, and they become truly free in Christ.

But then I've noticed something else...I noticed that when I've tried to enforce rules which aren't rooted in Scripture, they often go right back into bondage again." David's conclusion wasn't that principled guidelines aren't helpful at all, but that people can only truly be discipled through the *Word of God,* and that real change of behavior can only happen as the Holy Spirit transforms the affections *through the Word.* The goal of discipleship is the complete sanctification of the person, and this sanctification can only happen through the inspired text. It alone has the power.

Let Jesus live in and through you, love people, and never give in to fear.

From David I also learned that true holiness is best expressed not *merely* as "Christ*likeness*" but as the *"operation of the very life of Jesus within us through the Holy Spirit,"* manifesting then in Christ-like words and actions. He believes that "Christlikeness" could be misunderstood as merely *acting* like Jesus but without a transformed heart and mind. This insight has deepened my understanding of union with Christ and being indwelt by the Spirit.

I learned that love is the most important thing, and that ministry without love will only harden people's hearts to the truth. David taught me that love is more than words but meeting needs, sharing resources, and showing genuine concern for the people God brings into our lives. He is also a firm believer in church discipline, but discipline with love—discipline which offers forgiveness and a path to redemption.

I learned that a man-fearing spirit is the doorway to hypocrisy leading to a grieved Spirit.

David believes we must do what we do because it is right and because it pleases God. I've seen David and Margie turn down money and privilege because receiving them would cost their convictions.

Be practical and don't over-spiritualize the ministry.

I learned that prayerful, thorough, practical planning is critical to spiritual leadership, and that we should not over-spiritualize the ministry. David is a big-picture visionary, but I've learned so much from his attention to detail, whether he's teaching, managing a building project (usually multiple projects at once), conducting a service, or planning a Bible camp. For him, carelessness is a symptom of a spiritual problem that hinders the work of God. *Holy shoddy is still shoddy!*

I've watched David and Margie host countless Bible conferences. Well in advance of each conference, jobs are delegated, a theme is prayerfully chosen, speakers are assigned their topics, sound equipment is thoroughly checked, prayer, worship, and band members are selected (and directed to practice well), menus are carefully planned with consideration for the foods of the various tribes who will attend, experienced cooks are hired, even food lines are rehearsed for maximum efficiency. Rooms and surroundings are cleaned, water tanks are filled to the brim (something very important in their context), contingency plans are made for emergencies, etc. Nothing is taken for granted. Most importantly, David requires that every leader who takes part in the leadership of the conference, especially the speakers and worship team, spend time in fasting and prayer. (He's been known to even text the missionaries to ask if we've fasted and prayed for our topics, which has personally never offended me.)

David takes this thoughtful approach to everything he puts his hand to and trains his leaders to do the same. No stone is left unturned, because David believes in the direct connection between mindful, prayerful, diligent planning, and the favor of God upon our work. "For God is not a God of confusion but of peace. As in all the churches of the saints.... But all things should be done decently and in order" (1 Corinthians 14:33, 40).

David and Margie have both taught me the importance of hospitality. So much of the planning and organizing I just described is done to make God's people feel welcomed and as accommodated as possible. I've watched them treat each person as an honored guest, whether rich or poor, young or old, educated or illiterate, missionary or national. They do not do this because they want to win favor, but because they value each person as an image bearer of God, worthy of dignity and respect. They also do it to minimize distractions during conferences so that delegates might concentrate on the things of God.

Be sober but keep a sense of humor.

I also learned that one's word is one's honor. David can be shrewd, though he doesn't like it when we say so! Many of us remember how he's sometimes half-jokingly tried to get us to commit financially to projects, knowing that once we gave our word he'd have us "trapped!" He has little tolerance for casual promises. With playful seriousness, he and his pastors sometimes give nicknames to missionaries who make casual promises, names which correspond to their promise. One missionary said he wanted to purchase a bell for a church he visited, so they called him "Mr. Bell" for ten years until he delivered on his promise. One missionary was named "Mr. Tin Roof" and another "Mr. Deep Well"! It's all *very* funny, and David, when recounting these stories, always laughed the loudest.

David has taught me the importance of laughter. He sees humor everywhere, and has taught me that authentic Christianity, with its many burdens and crosses, will lead to a lightheartedness of faith.

we can laugh at ourselves. We can laugh at the many ironies of ministry. We can laugh at our mistakes. Laughter is great medicine. Sometimes, over the years, when David felt that he was getting on my nerves, which happened more often than you might imagine in some seasons, he'd say, "I know I'm heavy, Brother Tim, but if you truly love me, you'll carry me with joy!" I have!

He taught us the foolishness of urinating in our own drinking water!

Did I just shock you? Well, that's a tribal expression, and I've heard pastors and missionaries both howl with laughter when David reminds them of this! We know what he means. He means that we will have to drink the foolish consequences of our poor choices, so we should be very careful. All of us, including David, have had to drink our share of bitterness. The crass imagery has helped me on numerous occasions.

Be the first to humble yourself.

David taught me by his words and example that humility is the key to effective leadership. He said to me one day (I think it was when he sensed I was a little embarrassed by a poor message I had preached), "You know, Brother Tim, you can't humiliate a truly humble man." I confessed that I must still be a little proud, and we had a good laugh together!

But I watched him suffer. I watched him fail. I've watched him repent before his pastors and local congregation. I've watched him take responsibility for foolish choices. I've watched him come under authority and accept accountability. I've heard him many times confess to a season of spiritual barrenness. And I've witnessed grace poured into his life and into the ministry because of humility. I've watched him not only give but also *receive* rebuke and instruction. And because David leads the way in humility, the Lord is using him to form a culture of humility among his leaders.

Work with a vision.

David has taught me the power of faith and vision. I'll never forget the day in 1999 that he came to the Bible school campus where our family lived and pulled me aside. He was solemn, and I knew he had something very important to tell me. (Under his leadership, a few churches had been planted by this time, and we'd just completed a training center for training church planters in his hometown—a huge answer to prayer.) "During a recent season of prayer and deep meditation," he began, "I sensed the Lord clearly speaking to me, asking me what I would like to ask him for. And I've asked him for *a million souls for Christ!*" I believed him and poured myself into this vision with him—a vision which still inspires me today.

Some may dismiss this, but I can tell you that from that day until today the *vision for a million souls* has been the guiding light for everything Gospel Light ministries has planned, endeavored, and accomplished.

David has never made it about himself, but about God's grace. And neither David nor his pastors necessarily believe a million souls will be discipled in *their* lifetime; but they *do* believe that if they will be faithful to lay a strong foundation, future generations will build upon it until the vision is accomplished.

Never be intimidated by the devil.

David has taught me to respect, but not to fear demonic powers. He and his pastors have encountered countless overt manifestations of the enemy, armed with the Word of God, confidence in the gospel, and focused prayer, with fasting.

I was with David and several Gospel Light pastors in a village one night when a young girl was delivered from demonic oppression. Her relatives said she'd been in an unresponsive state for days. The presence of darkness all around her was strong. Her breathing was loud and unnatural, but we couldn't awaken her. So, we began to sing and pray over her in the name of Jesus. The whole church gathered as we praised God for the power of the blood of Jesus to save and deliver. Within thirty minutes, a wonderful peace filled the new little chapel, and the little girl woke up, looked around, asked for a drink, and then walked out of the room as if nothing had been wrong! These twenty years later she is still a witness to the power of the gospel in that place.

Lead the way in worship!

David demonstrates the priority of the Word of God in prayer and modeled for me a heart of worship. Those who've been around David will agree that if he's anything at all, he's a worshiper. He made a choice not to be self-conscious or half-hearted. He remembers the pit from which he's been dug.

I remember the day we visited a new church plant together. David led the service, and when it came time for the offering, he thought this would be a good time to instruct these new believers in giving. "When I come to worship our great God, I never want to come empty-handed or give a gift that costs me nothing. I always want to bring something to show my love and gratitude!" he said. And that's how he teaches. God's laws and God's ways are not burdensome, but a joy and a delight, because God is a joy and a delight.

To this day, nearly every time the offering plate passes, I think of this. Most of the time I don't carry cash anymore, and most of our giving is online, but I always check my heart. *Are Becky and I giving generously with a sense of devotion and gratitude?*

You need a true friend.

David has taught me the beauty of friendship. Not a sentimental friendship. He's taught me that true friends rebuke one another in love. He taught me that healthy friendships are rooted in Christ, and in truth and honesty. He said to me one day, "Brother Tim, our relationship must always be centered on our mutual love for Jesus—not money, not position, not race, or anything else. Natural friendships are based on these kinds of things, but when these things are gone the relationship is destroyed. If Jesus is at the center, our relationship will always be secure."

Find a friend like David.

David demonstrates the power of a godly mentor, and I count it one of the greatest blessings of my life that our lives have been woven together.

> Like deep rivers flowing quietly through the landscape of our world, there are deep, pure men and women flowing quietly through your life. But you must learn to see them, for they aren't always easy to recognize.

I've spent nearly 5,000 words telling you about my friend, simply to encourage you to find a friend. Look for people in *each season of your life* who are more advanced, more experienced, and more successful than you, and learn from them. Like deep rivers flowing quietly through the landscape of our world, there are deep, pure men and women flowing quietly through your life. The Lord has ordained it. He has placed them there for your benefit. But you must learn to see them, for they aren't always easy to recognize. You must learn to draw from their wisdom, for they're too humble to disperse their wisdom where it is not wanted or requested.

- Observe their lives.

- Learn from their example.

- Ask questions.

- Draw out wisdom.

- Listen.

- Be vulnerable.

- Don't be afraid to show weakness.

- Be teachable.

- Heed their warnings.

Sometimes you may want to ask that person to mentor you, but many times your relationship won't be formal at all. You can learn up close, and you can learn from a distance, but always learn. When I meet a person who must always be the smartest person in the room, I know I'm meeting a person who hasn't yet been broken. Be a learner.

KEEP AN ETERNAL PERSPECTIVE

Here's one final lesson I learned from David that I want to leave with you: *Live every day with eternity in view!*

A few years ago, Gospel Light dedicated a new campus for conferences and training, including an auditorium for 800, dormitories, and a guest house. It was a great day of celebration because almost everyone in attendance had done what they could to see this project completed. Gospel Light churches had taken offerings. Overseas workers and USA churches had contributed significantly as well. Farmers provided food for the workers. I remember one little lady, very poor, who donated sweet potatoes. Pastors and laypeople volunteered labor. It was a collective effort, with everyone doing what they could, and it made for such a joyful occasion.

David had managed the entire project, and I'll never forget the testimony he gave during the dedication service. As the work went on month after month, he said he would sometimes wonder how God was going to supply the needs. The work was slow, tedious, often tiresome, and a test of faith. "Very often as I managed the project," he said, "I would have to run to town for supplies, and as I traveled, I would sing a song to myself reminding myself of the importance of living each day, and doing each task, with eternity in view." And then he sang this song by Lanny Wolfe as his testimony:

> It matters so little
> How much you may own
> The places you've been
> Or the people you've known
> It all comes to nothing
> When placed at His feet

It's nothing to Jesus
Just memories to keep.

Only one life, so soon it will pass
Only what's done for Christ will last
Only one chance to do His will
So give to Jesus all your days
It's the only life that pays
When you recall you have but one life.

The days pass so swiftly
The months come and go
The years melt away
Like new fallen snow
Spring turns to summer
And summer to fall
Autumn brings winter
Then death comes to call

Only one life, so soon it will pass
Only what's done for Christ will last
Only one chance to do His will
So give to Jesus all your days
It's the only life that pays
When you recall you have but one life.

As I listened my eyes flooded with tears. I've met few people in my life who've lived with such focus, but this is how my friend, David, has taught me to live life. I hope you will live your life this way too. Start with a commitment to know God, especially as he's revealed in

Jesus, find spiritual rest in Christ's finished work, live with integrity, train yourself toward godliness, be humble, get a vision, work hard, love deeply, and find a friend—a friend like David.

NOTES

CHAPTER 1

1. https://moodyaudio.com/products/running-toward-your-calling-part-1
2. 2 Corinthians 12:7
3. A.W. Tozer, "God is the Most Winsome of All Beings" in *Renewed Day by Day (Volume 1)*. Retrieved from https://dailytozer.wordpress.com/2012/09/01/god-is-the-most-winsome-of-all-beings September 12, 2020

CHAPTER 2

1. Much of this section can also be found in *Spiritual Formation*, written by Tim Keep, and published by Shepherds Global Classroom, Lesson 2.
2. https://www.desiringgod.org/messages/summer-is-for-seeing-and-showing-christ
3. As stated by Dave Eubanks, founder of Free Burma Rangers.

CHAPTER 3

1 Dennis Kinlaw, *This Day with the Master,* (Zondervan, 2002), February 15
2 John Wesley, *Fifty-Two Standard Sermons,* "On Repentance in Believers"
3 From *Becoming Elisabeth Elliot,* by Ellen Vaughn
4 Dietrich Bonhoeffer, *Prison Poems*

CHAPTER 4

1 Charles Swindoll, Hand Me Another Brick, (Thomas Nelson, 2006) p.106
2 https://www.missionfrontiers.org/issue/article/15-mind-blowing-statistics-about-pornography-and-the-church

CHAPTER 5

1 John Wesley's notes on 1 Timothy 4:7
2 Dallas Willard, *Hearing God*
3 DA Carson, *For The Love of God,* Vol 2
4 Lettie Cowman, *Streams in the Desert* (Grand Rapids: Zondervan, 1996), June 11
5 The author believes he quoted this from Matthew Poole.
6 Arthur T. Pierson, *George Muller of Bristol*

CHAPTER 6

1 Mark 10:46-52
2 John Wesley

CHAPTER 7

No Notes

CHAPTER 8
1   NT Wright

CHAPTER 9
No Notes

CHAPTER 10
No Notes

ABOUT THE AUTHOR

TIM KEEP and his wife, Becky, have served in intercultural ministry for twenty-seven years, thirteen of those in the Philippines. In 2012 Tim founded Shepherds Global Classroom, a training ministry to underserved pastors and Christian leaders in dozens of countries. Tim and Becky have been blessed with 5 children and 5 grandchildren, and together have authored four books, including *Eyes to See: Glimpses of God in the Dark*, *It's All About Obedience: One Woman's Discovery of a Fruitful Life in a Foreign Land*, and *All is Well: Finding the Great Heart of God When a Child Walks Away*. Their books can be found at www.beckykeep.com.